SPACE BETWEEN PEOPLE

SPACE BETWEEN PEOPLE

EDITED BY STEPHAN DOESINGER

WITH CONTRIBUTIONS BY:

Drew Harry, Dietmar Offenhuber & Judith Donath
Matthias Böttger & Friedrich von Borries
Melinda Rackham & Christian McCrea
Maximilian Schich & Steffen Krämer
Pascal Schöning
Tor Lindstrand
Shumon Basar
Norman Klein
Mario Gerosa
Lester Clark
Kate Allen

PRESTEL

Munich   Berlin   London   New York

© Prestel Verlag, Munich ·
Berlin · London · New York,
2008

© of works illustrated refer
to picture captions, with the
exception of Le Corbusier,
Giorgio de Chirico, Yves Klein
by VG Bild-Kunst, Bonn 2008

Front cover image by
Tor Lindstrand

Prestel Verlag
Königinstrasse 9
80539 Munich
Tel. +49 (0)89 24 29 08-300
Fax +49 (0)89 24 29 08-335

Prestel Publishing Ltd.
4 Bloomsbury Place
London WC1A 2QA
Tel. +44 (0)20 7323-5004
Fax +44 (0)20 7636-8004

Prestel Publishing
900 Broadway, Suite 603
New York, N.Y. 10003
Tel. +1 (212) 995-2720
Fax +1 (212) 995-2733

www.prestel.com

Prestel books are available
worldwide. Please contact
your nearest bookseller or one
of the above addresses for
information concerning
your local distributor.

Library of Congress Control
Number: 2007943208

British Library Cataloguing-
in-Publication Data:
a catalogue record for this
book is available from the
British Library. The Deutsche
Bibliothek holds a record of this
publication in the Deutsche
Nationalbibliografie; detailed
bibliographical data can be
found under:
http://dnb.ddb.de

Translation by
Paul Aston, Rome
Editorial direction by Curt Holtz
Design and layout by
Stephan Doesinger, Munich
Design assistance:
Lisa Bartl, Dominik Maier
Origination by Christian Olsson
(www.olssongrafik.de), Munich
Printed and bound by MKT,
Ljublijana

Printed on acid-free paper

ISBN 978-3-7913-3991-7

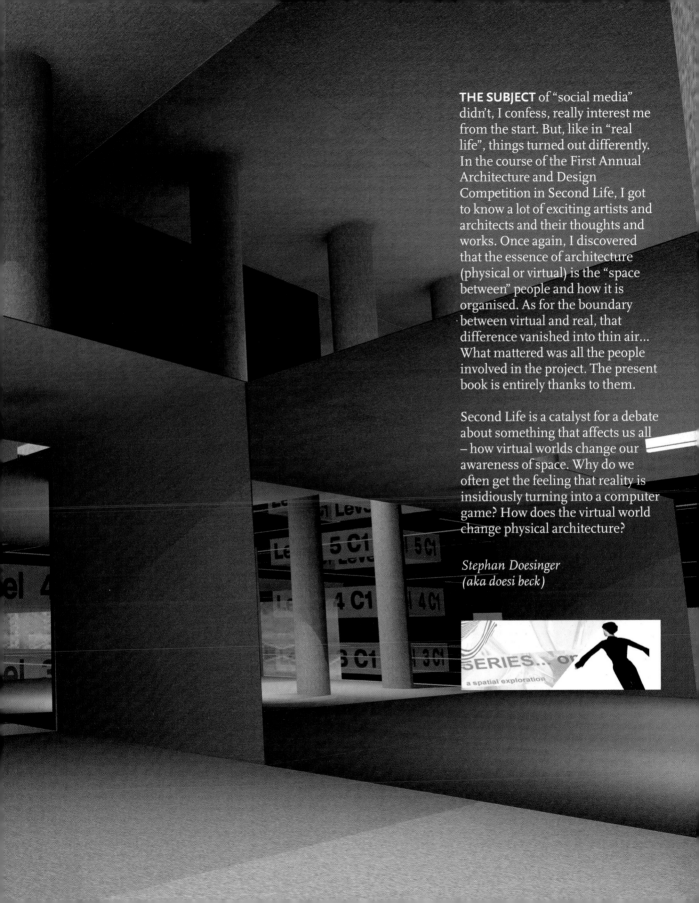

THE SUBJECT of "social media" didn't, I confess, really interest me from the start. But, like in "real life", things turned out differently. In the course of the First Annual Architecture and Design Competition in Second Life, I got to know a lot of exciting artists and architects and their thoughts and works. Once again, I discovered that the essence of architecture (physical or virtual) is the "space between" people and how it is organised. As for the boundary between virtual and real, that difference vanished into thin air... What mattered was all the people involved in the project. The present book is entirely thanks to them.

Second Life is a catalyst for a debate about something that affects us all – how virtual worlds change our awareness of space. Why do we often get the feeling that reality is insidiously turning into a computer game? How does the virtual world change physical architecture?

Stephan Doesinger
(aka doesi beck)

X: I remember that room very well... where you were waiting for me. Yes, there was a mirror over the chest; and it was in that mirror that I saw you first, when I opened the door without making a sound...

SPACE

BETWEEN

PEOPLE

X: *And once again I was walking on down these same corridors, walking for days, for months, for years, to meet you... There would be no possible stopping place between these walls, no rest... I will leave tonight... taking you away with me...*

A: –

*X: A year... You wouldn´t
have been able to go on
living among this trompe
l'oeile architecture, among
these mirrors and these
columns, among these
doors always ajar, these
staircases that are too
long... in this bedroom that
is alway open...*

**Last Year in Marienbad –
a story of constant persuasion.
Actress Delphine Seyrig in her
Coco Chanel dress.**

EXPLORING A NEW CONCEPT OF INSIDE AND OUTSIDE AND WHAT IT MEANS TO BE

VIRTUALLY HOME

— STEPHAN DOESINGER

Elements of space. © Annsunnyday | Dreamstime.com

ON INTERACTIVE COMPUTER GAMES

In 1997 we were invited to produce an art project in a well-known "techno" club in Munich in connection with a symposium on electronic music. We decided to recreate the premises of the club – including all the works of other artists exhibited there – in the 3D-modelling program of the Ego shooter game *Marathon*.[1] We installed numerous monitors and projectors on the spot in the real room, and allowed anyone to play who wanted to. The aim of this LAN (local area network) game was to kill aliens and other opponents with an arsenal of martial weapons. The aggressive situation required maximum alertness. Any distraction could mean your own virtual death. Real space merged into virtual space in front of our eyes. After the game, no one could go round the corner in the real room without some palpitations...

"Somehow I managed to escape the realm of the Ego-shooter Marathon..."

Even if LAN games are different from MMOG (massive multiplayer online games) such as Second Life in having other players simultaneously present in the room, while you remain anonymous and singular, the experiences we had are applicable to virtual worlds such as Second Life:

1) In the club there was a double floor that led to the loss of the genius loci, and gave rise to a new mental map.

"... only to wake up years later as a girly-avatar in a Second Life - radio show to give an interview..."

2) Our whole spatial perception was reduced to audiovisual elements. All other senses of spatial perception were largely blotted out. We realised that the success of AV "spatial creations" lies in them being easily controllable in comparison with the physical architecture.

3) The interaction generated an undertow that affected our thinking. As in driving a car, it gave us a restricted field of action that required total concentration and instinctive thinking. Associative thinking was replaced by instinct and quick reactions. Daydreaming when driving causes accidents.

"... later I was turned into a Peter Pan look-a-like-wanna-be to follow an invitation to give a talk at the London Design Museum..."

We soon realised that it's a myth to think that interactive spaces necessarily lead to more creativity. Quite the contrary – our experiment showed that the capacity for personal spatial ideas and intuition was inhibited. This is incidentally how interactive environments also differ from the classic cinema experience. Films create freedom for your own associations and memories by what they don't show and by what, like editing techniques, separates and links time and space. Here, the difference between gaming and playing is discernible. Playing has to do with inventing and is less rule-bound than gaming. In other words, you can only imagine what is not there. The more you show, the less the rest has to be imagined. The less you have to imagine, the easier you are to control.

ARCHITECTURE'S SECOND LIFE

What was missing from Second Life was the storyline. Unlike in *Marathon*, there was not even a target, a high score. No one understood what the game was about. So why all the media hype about Second Life? What's the plot in Second Life?

"I met various other artists who explained me the world..."

"But now?"

The answer is obvious – the narrative element of Second Life is reality itself. In Second Life, we look at a scene which is more than a metaphor for reality. It is both – reality and metaphor at the same time! Alongside the self-dramatisation by means of avatars and buildings as alter egos, it is about social adaptation. Put more precisely, Second Life is not about producing architecture or chatting about important things but about "playing at architecture" and "playing at communication".

In Second Life, stage sets are produced for an absurd theatre reminiscent of Robbe-Grillet's *Last Year in Marienbad*.[2] Three-dimensional self-portraits and dream houses come up if, like Jeff Bridges in *The Big Lebowski*, you fly over a landscape that oscillates aesthetically between Bob Ross and *The Sims*. Anyone who wakes up for the first time in the architecture of virtual exile is inevitably reminded of David Lynch's surreal scenario in *Lost Highway*.

Gaudy though the world in it seems, it is nevertheless affirmative. That is why most of the avatars look like Pamela Anderson and Brad Pitt, gestures are standardised, most of the buildings are ordinary suburban houses or fair stalls, and the whole space is a mimetic doll's house. Moreover, everything is there to play a role – as with a doll at the psychiatrist's. It is as if the architecture itself is lying on Freud's couch because in reality it is undergoing a serious identity crisis provoked by media-based spatial awareness. That is sufficient reason to examine the results of the first Architecture and Design Competition in Second Life.

As part of Ars Electronica in Linz, an international jury selected four winning projects from 126 submissions, and after a public vote prizes were awarded at the Zeche Zollverein in Essen. All the works came from professional architects and designers. The jury (Pascal Schöning and Shumon Basar from the London-based Architectural Association, Melinda Rackham of the Australian Network for Art and Technology, Tor Lindstrand from the Royal Institute of Technology in Stockholm and architectural curator Mathieu Wellner) focused on projects that were formally largely abstract, invited other users to get involved or were simply more exciting than reality.

So what reality might that be? What sort of reality is it where terms such as "mixed realities", "augmented realities", "virtual spaces", "hybrid spaces" or "the metaverse"[3] have become commonplace? In what form do these amorphous concepts reveal their importance for our reality and our awareness of space? What role does the aesthetic aspect have?

Numerous projects succumbed to the lure of a formal "anything goes", and let rip an orgy of forms. Unencumbered by static and commercial constraints, Sullivan's dictum that "form

"... I feel as if my creator has abandoned me...

*... but even worse -
I think I´m lost."*

"... hmm, and I am almost certain, that I am being observed...

Time to make a move!"

TV-Helmet, (Portable living-room),
1967 by Walter Pichler. Sculpture.
Polyester, varnished white, integrated
TV-monitor with TV-access,
59 x 120 x 43 cm.
© SAMMLUNG GENERALI FOUNDATION, VIENNA

follows function" seems to have degenerated into farce. What function could that be, anyway? What are the functions and effects of designs in virtual space?

By definition, virtuality specifies an imaginary entity or one made specific via its characteristics. Though it is not physical, it is present in its functionality or effect. Max Moswitzer's *White Noise* project tackled this notion by means of ironic detachment, which is also why the jury selected it. He compiled a constantly changing architecture from freely disposable elements called "freebies". Magnified three-dimensional everyday objects such as skateboards, bottles, transport vehicles, chairs, teddy bears and lots more shine white like skeletons. It is the result of a cheerful shopping round for shapes that subsequently, bleached out like dead coral, have a different story to tell. Inevitably one is reminded of a rubbish tip from Julian Opie's workshop. You sense an echo of figures from classical antiquity, whose virgin white has survived into modern architecture as a concept of beauty, even if we meantime have discovered that the figures were originally colourfully painted and decorated. *White Noise* is a neo-antique collection of objects whose graphics, skins and textures got lost on the way.

The technically most innovative projects largely ignore mimetic architecture and see themselves as three-dimensional interfaces. Meylenstein's project *Living Cloud* is a virtual house in the shape of a cloud that always surrounds you and changes as a result of social contact. However, the cloud also shrouds its avatar, thereby generating a small protective zone. In his *Seventeen Unsung Songs*, Adam Nash produced a lyrical garden of sounds whose elements change and generate sounds on contact. D C Spensely's project *Full Immersive Hyperformalism* is likewise a three-dimensional collection of interactive spots embedded in an orthogonal "space frame". It is one of those projects that foreshadow the future potential of virtual three-dimensional worlds as interfaces to real spaces. It is easy to imagine that they could function as intelligent remote controls for real spaces or like three-dimensional telephones. As with all Web 2.0-driven media, all projects involved something we might term "the virtual home".

WELCOME TO THE BASTARD SPACE

I launched this competition because, as a result of my own work in art[4], I came to the conclusion that computer games such as Second Life no longer just copy the world but a creeping inversion process is taking place. I am reminded of a comment by Walter Benjamin in 1929 that has perhaps become a central metaphor of our basic cultural situation these days:

"When two mirrors look at each other, Satan plays his favourite game and opens
a perspective on infinity." [5]

Our own position lies somewhere between these two mirrors looking at each other. We are permanently faced with reality and its images in the media, which mutually reflect each other. In the force field between these two poles, a new awareness of space is generated in which the absence of presence has become normal. Where are you actually when you ring from a mobile? What reality are you in when you have your iPod in your ear and the acoustic space is uncoupled from physical space? What space are you in when you play a computer game, surf the net or in the future take a GPS-linked electronic shadow with you as an

BASTARD SPACE MANIFESTO

DISCOTECTURE

- by Stephan Doesinger

23

- 1 -
THE WORLD IS A COMPUTER GAME
AND YOUR HEART BEATS LIKE POP CORN.

- 2 -
ARCHITECTURE IS THE SPACE BETWEEN PEOPLE.

- 3 -
THE ICONOGRAPHIC KILLS THE IMAGINARY.

- 4 -
BUILDINGS ARE OBSTACLES!

- 5 -
THE EARTH, A BLOOD CRUSTED DISCO BALL,
DRIVEN BY SATELLITES.

- 6 -
INSIDE AND OUTSIDE ARE REPLACED
BY THE TERMS "PULL" UND "PUSH"!

- 7 -
AMBITION AND ARTIFICIAL LIGHT ARE THE
STRONGEST BUILDING MATERIALS!

- 8 -
BASTARD SPACES ARISE WHERE PHYSICAL SPACE
MERGES WITH MEDIA SPACE.

- 9 -
PUBLIC SPACE IS A MEDIA CONSTRUCTION.

- 10 -
FILM IS SPACES IN TIME – ARCHITECTURE IS TIME IN SPACE.

- 11 -
BECOME THE NEEDLE OF A RECORD PLAYER,
SCRATCHING ALONG FACADES.

Yeah!
www.doesinger.com

*"... strange postings
everywhere you go..."*

avatar? That these are not minor questions is shown by the example of American GIs who said that when they shot at Iraqis with loud music in their headsets they felt like in an action film. Clearly they were occupying two spaces that emulsified with each other to create a new, distorted reality. How hard this parallelism and simultaneous irreconcilability of spaces can hit is also shown by the last telephone conversations from the World Trade Center on 11th September.

It would seem that wherever physical and media space fuse new spaces also evolve. They are spaces that are sometimes present, sometimes absent, but are generally mobile and roam across the continents at diverse speeds until they burst like soap bubbles – at the end of a phone call on the motorway.

Let's call them "bastard spaces"!

GOODBYE PRIVACY

What we describe as public space is the sum of all bastard spaces. Public space is largely a media construct involving an economy measured in purchasing power, production runs and viewing figures. Where there are cameras, where the assembled contents are edited, is the actual meaning of what we term public space. What did the voices of millions of people protesting against the Iraq war on the streets of our cities achieve in the face of Colin Powell's successful Photoshop fiction of virtual nuclear launching pads? A grainy satellite picture of scarcely recognisable vehicles was repeated so often until a fear-filled space was generated in the western hemisphere that ultimately led to a war where force was anything but virtual. Urban planning with bombs.

Unlike self-controlled bastard spaces such as telephones or iPods, whose space-generating power you manage yourself, the supervision of "public" space lies outside our own field of influence. It is media operators who have power over contents and broadcasting times. They are the architects of public space.

In public space, people become consumers, focus groups and "eyeballs".[6] Individuals can now set about putting themselves across publicly via MySpace, YouTube, Second Life and soon MyWorld as well – so as thereby to regain justification for their existence as political individuals. It is clear that this privately changes the meaning of the term for good, because anyone who puts himself into the media is exposed to observation and monitoring. Ars Electronica in Linz, which sponsored the first competition, has therefore focused strongly on the "goodbye privacy" theme this year.

ICONOMANIA

Let us therefore look back at the other side of Benjamin's mirror, contemporary architecture. As architectural theoretician Anthony Vidler puts it, it creates a feeling of the uncanny, seeming fretful and creating nowhere to establish a home. Manifestly, alienation is at work in modernism.[7] In the mirror image, we see a contemporary architecture that, as French author Michel Houellebecq critically observes, is only concerned to "erect shelves of the social supermarket".[8] What we have is contemporary architecture that is now vastly more subject to commercial considerations, as competition jury member Tor Lindstrand soberly summed up: "Excel has had a greater impact on contemporary architecture than Rem Koolhaas,

Zaha Hadid and Frank O. Gehry have managed together." [9] But it would be presumptuous to ascribe this development to architects, as fewer than 10 per cent of buildings in Germany are actually built by architects. What we have is a kind of *Sim City* – urban planning based on urban economic simulations, and individual buildings are stylistic variants optimised per square footage and classified as residential, commercial and industrial zones. Whereas private architecture largely takes root in amorphous settlements and gated communities, commercial zones in the city are shaped by iconographic iconoclasm. The efforts of star architects cannot escape this either, even if they want to. Their work is, in Guy Debord's phrase, categorised as "places-to-be" architecture or "cultural theme-parks". [10] The same process can be followed in the breakneck development of cities in the Middle East, Lagos and Shanghai. Iconographic towers, airports and artificial palm islands reminiscent of creative terraforming in Second Life are walk-in super-symbols – copy/paste architecture that is easy to locate on Google Earth.

"... I just love the world from above. It´s all so peacefull, so happily innocent..."

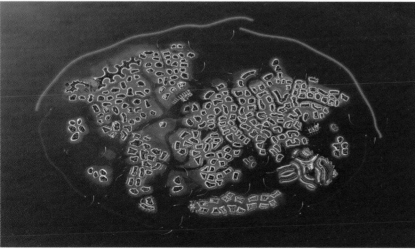

The future of Dubai is revealed in a never-seen-before rendering of what the city will look like from above in the coming years. It was released by Nakheel, the region's largest developer and a key force behind its most iconic developments, including world-famous man-made island The Palm Jumeirah.
© NAKHEEL
FROM THE PRESS TEXT
FROM NAKHEEL

"... and you should see the stuff on the ground – fantastically scripted objects and spaces..."

In 1972, in *Learning from Las Vegas: The Forgotten Symbolism of Architectural Form*[11], Izenour, Scott and Venturi described the iconography of the modern business city in terms of the Las Vegas Strip. They show how a city develops to accommodate cars. The function and message of a building should be immediately recognisable from the road. Six years later, the conclusion of Jean Baudrillard's "agony of the real" was that America had become Disneyland.[12] With the democratised view of the globe from the cosmos, one might add: Earth has become a computer game.

Looking at Google Earth has destroyed all the magic in the view of Earth that Neil Armstrong gave us. The image of Earth is in danger of getting worn out from over-use. John Berger's comment on this effect was that, if everything that existed were constantly being photographed, every photograph would become meaningless. The globe and all its cities are accessible from everywhere. From the screen, you can zoom from level to level, as in the Eames' *Powers of Ten*. It's only a few clicks from the real image of Darfur, New York or Kabul to a little home of your own somewhere on the three-dimensional playing field. In passing, you also see the urban zones that, as Mike Davis described in *Planet of Slums*,[13] are expanding most rapidly worldwide. In Google Earth, we experience a global exhibition every day without having anything to do with it. It is the extension of Malraux's idea of a museum without walls. It is a cool look at ourselves, with the detachment of a glance at an exhibit in the curio cabinet.

DOPPELGÄNGER

Back on the ground, we may note a strange transformation of the old architectural fabric. With the total marketing of cities (e.g. Edinburgh), even historic buildings become "branded builds" or Venturi's "decorated sheds" or "ducks". Particularly buildings that were hitherto vehicles of cultural identity become three-dimensional symbols of themselves at a 1:1 scale. The absurd thing is that, the more historic buildings are renovated and prettily floodlit, the more synthetic and alien they look. The Acropolis, Castel Sant'Angelo, Munich's City Hall, the Eiffel Tower or even less well-known buildings look like fakes with an artificial patina. The cultural substance of historic buildings is obscured by their plastic, stage-set appearance. Like an ephemeral graffito, the physical building acquires a spectacular doppelgänger that is disconcertingly beautiful and yet uncanny as well. [14]

Historic city centres are transformed into history lands with attached shopping malls. Behind them flourish, artificially air-conditioned, a similar range of shops in every city with branches of global brands from McDonald's to Gucci, bludgeoning shoppers with "functional music". Strangely enough, the artificial identity and alienation frequently associated with the concept of "urban periphery" thereby also creep into the heart of the city.

PUSH AND PULL

For Rem Koolhaas, shopping has become the final activity of mankind. Shopping zones are systems controlled down to the last detail, where nothing is left to chance. They are labyrinths with carefully choreographed orientation points – the products. The more time you spend in them, and the more convenience the space promises, the greater the turnover of goods. Convenience is another word for total control, but it is nonetheless perceived as pleasant because people are released from all responsibility for anything as long as their credit cards will stand it.[15] Airports are perhaps the best example of this because they are

What is the strongest building material – stone or light?
The illuminated pyramids of Giza constitute a space between fiction and reality. Light evokes not only a recollection of the scenery of a computer game. It also tells a new story: A 4,500 year old fragment of world heritage becomes a 3D icon in the global history theme park.

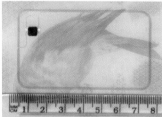

With one foot always in virtual space at the same time. E. g.: The radio frequency chip in a UK passport is a digital extension of the body that may soon become a 3D pendant in the shape of an avatar. Furnished with a GPS system, it makes us just as visible as all social networks, which are based on voluntary participation.

The effect is reminiscent of Foucault: *"The effect of surveillance is permanent even when the implementation is sporadic."*

transit areas and at the same time the shopping zones with the highest turnover per square foot. For art historian Max Schich, airports are liturgical areas with specific sequences and rituals, the purpose being the Eucharist. Secularised man experiences transubstantiation at the moment the plane's wheels leave the runway. It is not so very different with virtual spaces through whose corridors we can let ourselves be teleported motionlessly in every direction. Second Life provides the right picture for the narcissistic desire to fly. But before the traveller can take off at the airport, he has to pass through various checkpoints. Strict behavioural rules and guidance systems operate to channel him as quickly as possible from A to B.

Even so, he has to keep pausing and waiting – the underground garage, check-in, body check, baggage screening, finally finishing up in the duty-free zone. Restaurants and shops form an outlet to an apparent autonomy of controlled opportunities for choosing between KFC and Rolex. Both Second Life and airports are convenience spaces that deprive us of any responsibility. In Foucault's terms, these spaces are structurally reminiscent of a prison. But in contrast to "real" prisons, they are happy imprisonments because they operate not with repression but with seduction. In marketing, there are two fine terms, "push" and "pull". "Push" means the real prison you are warned against in American schools with the words: "Take responsibility for your life, or others will do it for you." In the worst case, people are told when to get up, what to put on, what to eat, etc. "Pull" means the immediate promise of happiness that can be redeemed by buying something. The greatest feeling of happiness is an almost infantile feeling of security when the responsibility of accepting responsibility is taken from you. And what for, anyway? Everything is only temporary, everything is flexible. One is oneself only a node in a loose network.

The spiritual link between virtual and real worlds is affected by portable media such as Blackberries, laptops, iPods, etc. These tools can best be seen as "spaces in transit". "Spaces in transit" are spaces we know that give us a feeling of home. Favourite music in your ears, and familiar names and pictures on the screen, form an emotional interior within a Teflon-coated external space. If you link the metaverse with the portable medium and a GPS system, your own body will always be accompanied by a digital alter ego. We carry our virtual homes around with us like snail shells. With a radio-frequency chip in our electronic or biometric passes (e-pass, electronic passport, eID), we are already carrying our virtual persona around with us, like an electronic shackle. The fully immersive three-dimensional variant is now in its genesis, with Orwellian potential.

In the second life of architecture, a new meaning for the terms inside and outside opens up to us shortly before takeoff. In bastard space, inside and outside become processes, because they involve a spatial awareness that is governed by the medium. As on a Möbius strip, the concepts of inside and outside are replaced by the terms attraction and repulsion, or "pull" and "push".

Surrounded by Benjamin's mirrors along the Möbius strip, eternity has already begun. But anyone who waits for the Resurrection in the second life of architecture hasn't understood anything. So how can one find meaning in all that, in the middle of Satan's favourite game? Perhaps we can find an answer in Italo Calvino's *Invisible Cities*, [16] in which he has the Great Khan looking up in his atlas the maps of cities that are threatened with nightmares and curses – Enoch, Babylon, Yahooland, Butua, Brave New World. In it, Kublai Khan says:

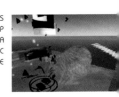

"It is all useless, if the last landing place can only be the infernal city, and it is there that, in ever-narrowing circles, the current is drawing us."

And Marco Polo:

"The inferno of the living is not something that will be; if there is one, it is what is already here, the inferno where we live every day, that we form by being together. There are two ways to escape suffering it. The first is easy for many: accept the inferno and become such a part of it that you can no longer see it. The second is risky and demands constant vigilance and apprehension: seek and learn to recognize who and what, in the midst of the inferno, are not inferno, then make them endure, give them space."

1 MARATHON IS A SCIENCE-FICTION FIRST-PERSON SHOOTER COMPUTER GAME PUBLISHED AND DEVELOPED BY BUNGIE SOFTWARE FOR THE APPLE MACINTOSH IN LATE 1994.

2 CF. LAST YEAR IN MARIENBAD BY ALAIN ROBBE-GRILLET, A CINE-NOVEL PUBLISHED BY JOHN CALDER, LONDON 1962. THE FILM WAS DIRECTED BY ALAIN RESNAIS IN 1960.

3 "THE TERM METAVERSE COMES FROM NEAL STEPHENSON'S 1992 NOVEL SNOW CRASH, AND IS NOW WIDELY USED TO DESCRIBE THE VISION BEHIND CURRENT WORK ON FULLY IMMERSIVE 3D VIRTUAL SPACES. THESE ARE ENVIRONMENTS WHERE HUMANS INTERACT (AS AVATARS) WITH EACH OTHER (SOCIALLY AND ECONOMICALLY) AND WITH SOFTWARE AGENTS IN A CYBER SPACE, THAT USES THE METAPHOR OF THE REAL WORLD, BUT WITHOUT ITS PHYSICAL LIMITATIONS." HTTP://EN.WIKIPEDIA.ORG/WIKI/METAVERSE.

4 CF. STEPHAN DOESINGER, LEARNING FROM SIM CITY, FRANKFURT 2007. "THE WORLD IS A COMPUTER-GAME AND YOUR HEART BEATS LIKE POP-CORN."

5 WALTER BENJAMIN, PARISER PASSAGEN (1929), IN: VOL. 5, WALTER BENJAMIN: GESAMMELTE SCHRIFTEN, ED. BY ROLF TIEDEMANN, FRANKFURT 1989.

6 "WE ALL SWIM IN AN OCEAN OF MASS MEDIA THAT FILLS OUR MINDS WITH PEOPLE AND EVENTS WITH WHICH WE HAVE NO ACTUAL CONTACT AT ALL. WE COMMONLY ABSORB THESE MEDIA PRESENCES AS PART OF OUR OWN 'REALITY,' EVEN THOUGH ANY MEDIA EXPERIENCE CONSISTS ONLY OF ONE-WAY, EDITED REPRESENTATIONS OF REALITY." MARK HOSLER, QUOTED IN: "SUITS, LAWSUITS AND ART: NEGATIVLAND TAKES ON THE MAN", BY DEUCE OF CLUBS, IN: PLANET MAGAZINE, JULY 4, 1995.

7 CF. ANTHONY VIDLER, THE ARCHITECTURAL UNCANNY, CAMBRIDGE, MA 1992.

8 CF. MICHEL HOUELLEBECQ, DIE WELT ALS SUPERMARKT, INTERVENTIONEN, COLOGNE 1999.

9 CF. "EXCEL HAS HAD A GREATER IMPACT ON CONTEMPORARY ARCHITECTURE THAN REM KOOLHAAS, ZAHA HADID AND FRANK O. GEHRY HAVE MANAGED TOGETHER." TOR LINDSTRAND, IN: "ARCHITECTURE'S SECOND LIFE", ARCHINECT, JANUARY 9, 2007.

10 GUY DEBORD, "RECUPERATION: THE AFFIRMATION OF SUBVERSIVE METHODS THROUGH THE SPECTACLE.", THE SOCIETY OF THE SPECTACLE, TR. DONALD NICHOLSON-SMITH, NEW YORK 1995, P.12–3. FIRST ENGLISH EDITION 1970; FRENCH ORIGINAL 1967.

11 "THE DUCK IS THE SPECIAL BUILDING THAT IS A SYMBOL; THE DECORATED SHED IS THE CONVENTIONAL SHELTER THAT APPLIES SYMBOLS." IN ROBERT VENTURI, DENISE SCOTT BROWN AND STEVEN IZENOUR, LEARNING FROM LAS VEGAS: THE FORGOTTEN SYMBOLISM OF ARCHITECTURAL FORM (REVISED EDITION), CAMBRIDGE, MA 1977, P. 87.

12 "DISNEYLAND IS THERE TO CONCEAL THE FACT THAT IT IS THE 'REAL' COUNTRY, ALL OF 'REAL' AMERICA, WHICH IS DISNEYLAND.... DISNEYLAND IS PRESENTED AS IMAGINARY IN ORDER TO MAKE US BELIEVE THAT THE REST IS REAL, WHEN IN FACT ALL OF LOS ANGELES AND THE AMERICA SURROUNDING IT ARE NO LONGER REAL, BUT OF THE ORDER OF THE HYPERREAL AND OF SIMULATION. IT IS NO LONGER A QUESTION OF A FALSE REPRESENTATION OF REALITY (IDEOLOGY), BUT OF CONCEALING THE FACT THAT THE REAL IS NO LONGER REAL, AND THUS OF SAVING THE REALITY PRINCIPLE." JEAN BAUDRILLARD, SIMULATIONS, NEW YORK 1983, P. 10.

13 MIKE DAVIS, PLANET OF SLUMS, NEW YORK 2006.

14 "THE UNCANNY IS WHAT ... USED TO BE HOMELY AND FAMILIAR – IT'S THE SECRETLY FAMILIAR THAT HAS BEEN DRIVEN OUT AND NOW COME BACK." SIGMUND FREUD: "DAS UNHEIMLICHE" (1919), IN: GESAMMELTE WERKE, VOL. XII, FRANKFURT 1999, PP. 227–278. "WE REALISE THAT IT IS THE FACT OF REPETITION THAT MAKES THE OTHERWISE HARMLESS WEIRD AND NOW IMPOSES THE IDEA OF INESCAPABILITY AND OMINOUSNESS. ... THE DOPPELGÄNGER HAS BECOME A NIGHTMARE VISION, JUST AS THE GODS BECOME DEMONS AFTER THE FALL OF THEIR RELIGION."

15 "IN 1967, IN A BOOK ENTITLED THE SOCIETY OF THE SPECTACLE, I SHOWED WHAT THE MODERN SPECTACLE WAS ALREADY IN ESSENCE: THE AUTOCRATIC REIGN OF THE MARKET ECONOMY WHICH HAD ACCEDED TO AN IRRESPONSIBLE SOVEREIGNTY, AND THE TOTALITY OF NEW TECHNIQUES OF GOVERNMENT WHICH ACCOMPANIED THIS REIGN." GUY DEBORD, COMMENTS ON THE SOCIETY OF THE SPECTACLE, NEW YORK 1990, P. 2.

16 ITALO CALVINO, INVISIBLE CITIES, NEW YORK 1974, P 165.

RULES FOR MIGRATION
AFTER THE BIRDS GO EXTINCT

– NORMAN M. KLEIN

We imagine the future, probably inaccurately: In the future, let us say a hundred years from now, most species of birds go extinct. That is what many predictions suggest. Wetlands for birds also disappear, having little purpose. In broader terms, for most human beings who live above the lumpen mass, the meaning of flight itself has changed entirely. Instantaneity has dissolved all distances. That means: whether we travel or stand still, we never leave, only arrive. This may sound grim, but not more alienating than before. The world did not fall to pieces because it lost variety. But the way it fell lacked the drama that we expected. The full-bodied apocalypse came like an overnight delivery; it fell short somehow. We look around, and see more of what was. All pods and polished cityscapes serve much the same food. Public life, in its modernist sense, has all but vanished, as promised, even if cities continue.

For those with some means (the so-called "middle class", an old term that lingers), what used to be solid has finally melted into air. You order objects and services; it follows, often with colossal errors, but without much oversight. Nothing that we once called solid flies as it used to, from place to place. Shipping, hauling, manufacture, armies – all heavy lifting resembles shipping containers more than industrial chaos. The factories are increasingly enclaved like those that were common in southern China in 2009. In the language of 2008, we fly only from brand to brand. But more crucial: the only migratory patterns that we literally experience – the clearest sense of difference – move inside our heads. One could say: like a game, like a second life. That has become the rule of business in 2117, to multi-task all sense of place. Thus, to stay current and keep our service jobs, the best jobs, we mentally slip from one parallel world to the next, like businessmen lost in a Phillip K. Dick novel.

Or perhaps not "lost": let us say adapted, in a Darwinian sense. "It could be worse" has become the most repeated proverb, according to a recent poll. With relatively little sense of historical difference – and no great interest in the future – even the present will not migrate forward. This is a future projected directly from our moment, in 2008 (I am writing in December 2007). A hundred surprises will turn this future on its head, I suppose. But a few constants will not go away. They are the foundation for the appeal of Second Life, however long that fad lasts. There will be, in fact already are, dozens already like it – sim environments, scripted spaces, parallel worlds as multi-user fantasies.

So, if I cannot guarantee that this scenario is accurate, let me at least project from our immediate past, to find what directions are inescapable. It is clear when our era began, even when our future began – a reasonably clear why. I will review these, then return to this scenario, to see what it can tell us. How we misremember the future is extremely revealing. That is essentially the scenario promised for generations now; once the iPhone has gone into its fortieth generation... Of course, the tools for slipping from world to world will come mostly out of computer programs (even God may be a pink light software from outer space, as P.K. Dick believed later in his life).

WHAT ARE THE PRE-HISTORIES OF SECOND LIVES?

Clearly, there were avatars and residents in second-life formats long before 2003. But to find a history of these, we need more than, for example, a timeline of multiple-user games since 1966. We need more surgical tools, more than a history of soft landings in games.

Let us try out an alternative: a history of the role of the viewer. We need to understand how a scripted-space model of the viewer has come to replace the older industrial versions. At which point historically does the viewer begin to literally enter as a central character in the story – inside electronic media, or inside shopping environments? Clearly, we are talking about the last fifty years. The pattern is quite plain to see, in the history of the shopping center, in the design of the fifties television screen, in the TV commercial talking directly to the viewer. We can easily pull back centuries earlier as well, to Baroque immersive environments, to the navigation of the viewer inside the painted dome, the scripted spaces that I discuss in *The Vatican to Vegas*.

Even more traditionally, going back to the fifteenth century, what remained of medieval carnival was also a second life, for a few days every year. There were seemingly endless variations on carnival, feast of fools – second-life festivals – held every year in Europe, even into the early nineteenth century. The purpose of these collective games was the world turned upside down, to reenact social conditions through playful inversions (the king of carnival as a peasant, etc.).

Then we find dances of death that were common in fourteenth and fifteenth-century Europe, another very different second life. In Munich, a dance of death as animated sculpture repeats on the famous clock every hour. Here, the imaginary blood is on the ground, like jousting, medieval and later Baroque point-and-shoot games. The struggles within the culture are theatricalized.

At last, a more surgical tool becomes obvious. Second-life games are standard in every culture. They are versions of the ludic impulse – of collective play. The games must deliver parallel worlds as cheerful nightmares. Outwardly, they are utopias, but what is a utopia? It is what can be built after all hope is gone, after nothing is worth saving. Utopias are indeed pathologies in reverse, darker than they seem, filled with collective paranoid repression, in order to keep the utopian spirit alive. Second life games must appear innocent as utopias, even naïve, like a communitarian love feast among comrades and neighbors. But underneath, the pleasure remains that they are pathologically dangerous worlds. They are the war of all against all. They emphasize their community of friends, in order to still be games, journeys into calculated risk, into hazard.

These journeys tend toward stories that may have a taste of drama (about character), some eyeliner that is epic (about worlds trembling, waiting for you to save them). But most of all, second lives are role-changing inside an imaginary society. They are social rituals about power. Inside these rituals, every friend is a potential enemy. That is the fun of the game, to destroy your friends. These are power struggles about unreliable social identities, about hierarchies up for grabs.

I remember as a teenager playing Monopoly with my friends for fifteen hours at a time. Each week, the rules would be shifted slightly, according to where our raging hormones were, about women, about the hunt for monopolies as the hunt for the future as we saw it. It was great fun to destroy each other's future, as a game, to bankrupt your friend, to threaten him.

The power struggles must be very precisely detailed. And the details must be updated regularly, kept up to the minute. That is the eerie fun – that your avatar and its property are weirdly or comically "like the real world" in every detail – at least in your conversations, in the chatter.

At any moment, these details can change. In fact, they ought to change; they should not be stable. Rules should respond to how economic power shifts places; or how your community changes its rules. Otherwise, second-life games lose their bite. In the US by 2010, as our social infrastructure inside cities and in our national government continues to change rapidly, Second Life will have to evolve new twists. As a ludic game, power must constantly grow new perversities. (For example, in those Monopoly marathons, we always twisted the rules about buying properties and suffering debts. Inside these special rules were anxious conversations about nuclear war, or puberty, jokes about parents who were Holocaust victims.) Second lives are tutorials about power relations that constantly change. They teach the viewer how to pretend to adapt. They are also games as collective safety valves. They are also imaginary acts of collective sadism – ways to take revenge, to transfer your anger on to someone else, and get away with it. This transference – the war among avatars – gives second lives a political scenario. They make sense of oligarchies and cruel systems of power at a given moment. Avatars must be cheerful, but ruthless. They not only transfer rage; they also split into two personae, or morph into each other's body. They pose as a harmonious utopia, in order to strike like mercenaries in Iraq.

Now let me narrow this prehistory: how did media second lives evolve after 1955? By media, I mean TV, or consumer spaces, shopping centers, even table games like Monopoly. Far more than Hollywood or live theater before 1955, TV talk invites the viewer to play god and the evil landlord. From 1955 to the late sixties, consumer-driven forms of audience participation appear on TV, or in shopping centers. These forms do not change much until late in the seventies. But already, after 1973, as globalism transformed the rules of power, these old formats looked increasingly out of place. At least, they did to me. Much of the sixties revolt was dedicated to imagining new forms of utopian play, new modes of installation, of performance theater. Inevitably new second-life formats would follow as well, particularly scripted spaces and multiple-user games. But the background – the context for this change – deserves a separate heading.

THE HISTORY OF THE PRESENT

That is a term very much identified with Foucault. Before a revolution takes place (i.e. The French Revolution) there are institutions where the reality of this revolution is already being acted out, even as play – ideology as play, imaginary madness, and the body and public torture as ideology. The present begins as theater, also as secret history – of governance before the fact.

I am currently building a history of the present for 2009. I will interview hundreds of people, and complete the book soon after the new president takes office. I have tried to locate a date when governance shifted toward "the present" at various institutions in the West, when the theater of the present began – before the fact of the post Cold War (1989, etc.), before the bad faith after 9/11. Clearly what is widely called globalism lay at the heart of this early, precognitive collective play, this shift in how capitalism was played. And clearly, this can be seen in mass culture by the late seventies in various computer games, in immersive

S
P
A
C
E

special effects cinema – and in larger events, like the digitalization of the banking industry, or the challenge of OPEC to western oil interests (or rather, how the NATO economy of the sixties changed directions in the seventies, without losing power really, simply expanding into new modes of game theory, let us say). It was clear in the emergence of Muslim fundamentalism (Iran), in Thatcherism to Reaganism, in the appearance of CNN, and new ways to merchandise (and control) the news in the US, in the growth of Japanese capitalism, in the new software and transistor designs that filtered out of NASA engineering, in the Arpanet leading to the Internet, and so on.

The date of this present is easy enough to fix. In the early seventies, a deep recession took hold of the US, as Nixon took power, as the war in Southeast Asia expanded, while Nixonian spin suggested that he was busily winding down the war. By 1973, the recession lifts, and the oil crisis begins, with the Yom Kipper war in October. The present begins, at least as prologue. We even have Ernst Mandel's warnings in the early seventies, about Late Capitalism. But the implications took decades to emerge. Indeed, late capitalism for whom? Not for East Asia. The sense of the shift for the West is implacable, in science fiction, in f/x movies, in the growing panoptical look of gated communities in the eighties. In the US, the highest point in the growth of the postwar middle class begins to drift downward after 1973.

HOME ENTERTAINMENT AND COMMUNICATIONS

Finally, between 1977 and 1992, the global economy – roughly speaking Western Europe, North America, and East Asia – brought forth thousands of new cultural tools, often as friendly "space" invaders, as cute weapons. Even a partial list is staggering, and all within a decade or so: the home computer; cable TV; digitized banking and warfare; home video and cell phones; themed post-urban cities; nano toys and games; genetic engineering; immersive architecture and cinema; simulation as fundamentalist politics.

By 2008, as Americans crash into the next era, reasonably informed consumerati "know the score". Polls indicate that most Americans are generally fed up by the so-called promise, the dividends after the end of the Cold War. They understand the risks very clearly, and are going into a collective nervous breakdown about it. Postmodern entertainment had essentially brought the long-promised society of control by way of simulation; nothing late about this capitalism. Power through media used entertainment to appear "user friendly", but it was as brutal as mid-nineteenth-century capitalism.

At the same time, the heritage of the eighteenth-century Enlightenment dissolved. Even in major cities, five-hundred-year distinctions between public and private identity mostly disappeared. And inside the old NATO alliance, the Euro-American nation state is dissolving into electronic feudalism.

Other than that, global coffee indeed tastes better, and labor is cheap (until it gets expensive). As a trade-off, post 1989 was the golden age of home entertainment; and an Olympian moment for good medication, for pharmacology guaranteeing Viagra hard-ons and a sugary personality. Most of all, it is a tragicomedy. A hundred years from now, children will dress as Americans for Halloween.

No surprise, then, that in the midst of the largest real-estate boom in decades, the illusion of safe investment and safe future should appear as Second Life in 2003. And that Second

Life should turn into real commodity investments so quickly, like sub-prime real-estate loans going from theater to chaos in 2007. There is endlessly in the US business talk of "soft landings". In the US, despite political agonies, the collapse has been ergonomic, user-friendly, filled with second lives. Home entertainment turned degeneration into media theater. It made special-effects movies about unearthly exploitation, about aliens with great computers taking over. In their movies, Americans were shown almost cheerfully colonized by their own economy; but the result, in fact, in the actual first life, proved as brutal and clumsy as a field surgeon sawing off limbs during the Civil War.

Even now, the cultural damage is mostly ignored (the shock to film, literature, theater, the fine arts, architecture, philosophy). From cable news to blogs to print, the cultural criticism also tends to be unfocused (even with the Bush era ending). I often call this moment "trying to scream while inside the stomach of the dragon". Our material culture has been anesthetized on a scale that crusader popes and fascist dictators would have envied.

It is equally clear that this earmarks the end of the city as we have understood it, far beyond the City Of Bits models of the 1990's, or the trans-local models. How strange though for us to visit this post-urban city, as first life: The buildings are as deodorized as computer graphics; the cultural tourism feels like an interface. We bring the true public life along with us, in our cell phones and our iPods; and in a few years, in our Kindle books.

We remember the legend of the turtle on a leash, or the lobster on a leash – the stories about modernity in Baudelaire's Paris. Now, the turtle is a cell phone; or perhaps, we are the turtle, taken for a walk by ourselves. Cultural tourism in the new city after cities indeed turn the first life into a second life, a scripted space where public life is strictly private. As I often mention in articles and lectures, we become tourists in our own city, and then inside our own body. Of course, beneath all this theater fantasy, second lives cloak the viewer, as if a Wagnerian opera. We are made invisible against the racism, the classism, the ruthless disregard, massive poverty, and political erosion. In second lives, all social afflictions are playful challenges. They reenact how identity changes when power is re-distributed. They are object lessons to the history of the present.

Second lives are always strangely plastic, in the original meaning of plastic, circa 1908 – endlessly flexible, wonderfully artificial. As the poet Apollinaire might have put it, second lives contain "purity, unity, and truth" that replaces nature itself. Apollinaire imagined those plastic unities as Cubism. Indeed, the computer may be the realization of Cubist design. But Apollinaire underestimated how social ritual and theatrical simulations of power can be plastic; and what indeed, they said. They are indeed plastic.

Modernist theories on playful theatrical second lives – as manifestations, happenings – point toward the endless dilemma. As a culture collectively senses its crisis, it settles into theater rather than action. Second lives are like naps in the middle of a train wreck. And as an inveterate daydreamer myself, I understand the impulse. But the history of the present that makes second lives possible, the theater as prologue to the crisis, is even more fascinating to me. Second lives are precognitive play, hints of what is to come; but never accurately enough, never predictions. I wonder what they are suggesting about the social relations that will be the basis of the next massive crisis, perhaps in the next ten years, or the next century, when whatever it was finally goes extinct.

UT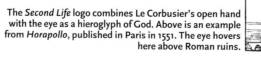PIA

SECOND LIFE

– STEFFEN KRÄMER AND MAXIMILIAN SCHICH

The *Second Life* logo combines Le Corbusier's open hand with the eye as a hieroglyph of God. Above is an example from *Horapollo*, published in Paris in 1551. The eye hovers here above Roman ruins.

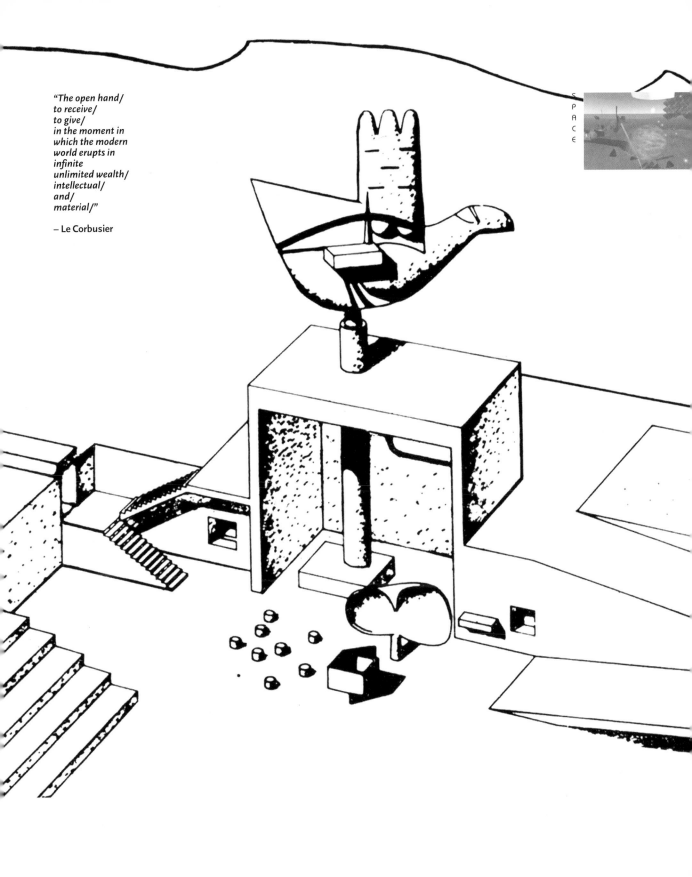

"The open hand/
to receive/
to give/
in the moment in
which the modern
world erupts in
infinite
unlimited wealth/
intellectual/
and/
material/"

– Le Corbusier

Complexity and Convention
by Maximilian Schich

N othing comes out of nothing"[1] is how art historian Ernst Gombrich once summed up the notion that in art history there are no developments without antecedents. Second Life is a development of that kind. The roots of this "virtual" world in fact go back to things that are often extraneous to the digital world people so readily describe as a new kind of medium, either to set themselves up as prophets of the new or to find an excuse for ignoring the subject. If you look at Second Life naively as an outsider – which is just what we are doing here – your view may initially be distorted according to your morality.[2] But if you take a wider view of Second Life or the phenomenon of simulated virtual 3D spaces as a whole, some useful insights can be gained relative to the history of art.[3]

In the present essay, we explore a number of characteristics of Second Life in pictures and words, convinced that the insights they reveal will be interesting for users as well as from an art-historical point of view. As is pointed out more than once in this book, Second Life is reminiscent of a utopia, i.e. an artificially created or imaginary ideal world. In fact, Second Life is an environment constructed by man. But in contrast to many historical utopias we shall go into in more detail, it is not only ideal or simple. Second Life often looks incomprehensible as well, apparently chaotic and complex. Ultimately, Second Life is both utopia and reality, simple and complex, beautiful and ugly, trivial and interesting.

The complexity of Second Life is easily explained. Instead of being defined by a single author or handful of authors, Second Life is the result of a variable application of the minimal definition of its basic components. Instead of creating a world, users produce individual parts of an environment with the help of a limited vocabulary, the interaction of which produces complexity that, at least superficially, increasingly comes to resemble the real world. As in other systems, for example the metabolism of a cell, traffic in the street or stock-exchange trading, here too global complexity arises as a consequence of activity at a local level.[4]

That is in stark contrast to the classic utopia. Unlike the visions of many an architect, no central idea is imposed on users of Second Life. In fact, as a result of the local activity of so many participants, there is a global dynamic and structure that can be controlled by individuals or a central authority only to a limited extent or not at all. As in a real state, it is necessary to adapt certain rules to actualities.[5] The actualities cannot be fixed in advance. Universal altruism and omnipresent rationality are for example just as utopian in Second Life as in real life.

Despite the inherent complexity arising from the interaction of the participants, large tracts of Second Life look dead. It never attains the density of the morning rush hour or a really good party, for example. Thinly populated is the normal state of things in Second Life, and there are no exceptions. Time and again, the scene looks like familiar pictures from all sorts of periods – the utopias from Urbino, Piranesi's prisons or de Chirico's squares. Like Archigram's *Gallery Project* we feel lost in a cacophony of shape and colour.

Why this absence of density? Like any man made thing, Second Life is based on various

Giovanni Battista Piranesi:
Carceri d'invenzione, Untitled
(The Staircase with Trophies)
(2nd state), etching, ca. 1750.
Disoriented we navigate
through the labyrinth of
invention. The wide angle
of view confirms our
imprisonment in the cartesian
precision of construction.

Giorgio De Chirico: Piazza d'Italia con sole spento, 1971, oil on canvas. Imagine you are looking at an empty Italian square, isolated architecture and a monument you don't understand. Promising landscapes appear in the distance. You switch off the sun. Bored – but metaphysical indeed.

Anonymous. Ideal City, oil on panel, around 1480 (Walters Art Gallery, Baltimore). Clarity results from perfect isolation of basic building archetypes, like the palace, the amphitheatre, the arch or the octagon. The tyranny of the geometrical does not allow for dirt, irregularity or ultimately life.

conventions, i.e. agreements between the authors that set up a limited frame of reference. Probably Second Life's most important deviation from real life in this frame of reference derives from the technical infrastructure: With the assistance of a large number of server computers, Second Life simulates the three-dimensional "grid".[6] Each server in the group is responsible for an area of 256 m squared, defined as a "sim" (as in simulation). All objects represented in this grid space are made up of pre-defined primary forms, called "prims". The number of prims per area is currently limited to 15,000. As the representations of users ("avatars") are likewise treated as prims, these are also subject to this limitation.[7] There is thus a direct proportionality of the simulated area to the maximum number of objects and also the number of people present at the same time. If the number of people and objects is to be increased, you can get round it to some extent, like the winner in the competition, but ultimately the area needs additional servers to cope.

Reality transcends into the sky: Andrea Pozzo's ceiling fresco in the Church of Sant'Ignazio in Rome. The windows and the arch on the far left are real. The architecture above is as virtual as the painted sky. And there is no gravity for the cloud of St. Ignatius.

Reality escapes from the grid. The Roman city of Thamugadi was initially laid out as a grid by the Emperor Trajan and then grew organically outside the walls.

In real life, for example in our cities, there are no such limitations to the growth of density. Instead of getting slower and slower, there is proof for the fact that our cities speed up with increasing size and density, the more people find their way into them.[8] As this density is not achievable in Second Life in the current configuration, large tracts of the simulated space look magically empty, like the above-mentioned utopias or the scenes in *Last Year in Marienbad* in the essay by Stephan Doesinger.

Even clearer is the difference from real life in Second Life's frame of reference if you look at the underlying conventions against a background of other representational spaces. Before Steffen Krämer goes further into the relationship between Second Life and well-known utopias, we shall therefore take a closer look at a number of important definitions of the convention – the space as a grid and the addressability of the prims as building blocks of the world.

Le Corbusier, *Vers un architecture*, Paris 1923. The modern architect identifies geometric primary bodies as the foundation of Roman Architecture in an ideal view of the ancient city.

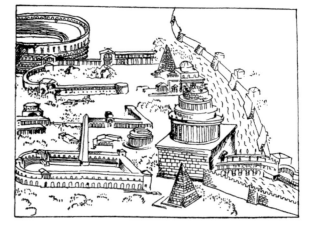

To define the space as a grid, i.e. a three-dimensional system of coordinates, it is important to note that this is an invention that is not as universal as it may seem in the age of GPS and Google Earth. In the western tradition, the roots of the idea of space as a grid go back at least to the fifteenth century, and are closely connected with the development of central perspective and other representational techniques.

Albrecht Dürer, Nude Figure Design, c. 1506, Sächsische Landesbibliothek, Dresden. Geometry can be used to idealise the proportions of a body. Deviation from the rule brings the figure to life. Numbers enable us to find the figure among similar ones.

As in Second Life, the various notations of three-dimensional grids are the result of a convention in the real world as well. In both cases, the convention allows us to refer to space beyond the boundaries of what is immediately visible. In David Summer's term, it defines a meta-optical space that can be depicted with geometrical precision.[9] The difference between the convention in Second Life compared with reality is that the latter exists without an imaginary system of coordinates. Second Life consists of the grid. Without the grid, it loses its basis.

If we compare the grid of Second Life with a classical Roman town plan, the consequences of this limitation become clear. Second Life is trapped within the walls of its own convention like an orthogonally arranged city. Everything that exists in Second Life must be oriented to the infrastructure of the sims. Large structures such as a theatre can embrace several units of area (i.e. sims or "insulae") but always remain convention-bound within the walls. It remains to be seen whether the publishers of Second Life are able to tear down these walls. Undoubtedly there will be conventions by third parties that will possibly allow freer handling of space, as in the case of the expansion of our classical city.[10]

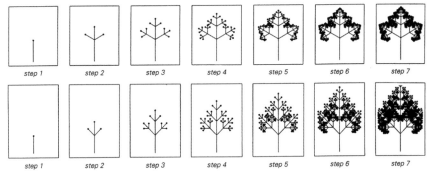

| step 1 | step 2 | step 3 | step 4 | step 5 | step 6 | step 7 |

| step 1 | step 2 | step 3 | step 4 | step 5 | step 6 | step 7 |

Stephen Wolfram, *A New Kind of Science*, Champaign/IL, 2001:
The complex growth of plants depends on very few variables. A tiny difference in one of those variables, like the branching angle, results in a totally different phenotype.

Among the pre-defined 'prims' in Second Life are on the one hand simple basic geometrical bodies such as cubes, cylinders, prisms or spheres, but other much more complex objects are also defined as basic shapes – i.e. "avatars", which are constructed from a network of triangles, and "plants", which are basically different from all other forms, but still relatively simply defined by a set of variables.[11] Every object in Second Life that is made up of one or more such prims is allocated a unique 16-byte character string in order to make it addressable.[12] This convention enables all components of Second Life to be kept perfectly discrete. Any fluid continuity is an illusion of projection. This is in stark contrast to our real world, which is conceivable as both discrete and continuous, and where the subdivision into objects is generally ambivalent and subjective.[13]

Ultimately, in its present form Second Life is not a world of its own but only another conventional form of representation just like for example 19th-century landscape painting[14] or any other form of art. Avatars are constructed like Dürer's Venus, architecture can be assembled of geometric bodies like Roman architecture in the eyes of Le Corbusier, and we can move in it like the inhabitants of the Villa dei Misterii in Pompeii or the dolls in a Neapolitan crib.

Regardless of which way Second Life or its successors develop, unlike reality we shall always realise that it is a simulation.[15] If we fail to recognise that distinction, the simulation simply becomes reality.

As a representational convention Second Life is a subject of art research, just as valid as any other. However, the jury's decision concerning the architectural composition has already shown that the familiar categories of real architecture such as high-rise building or residential building in Second Life make no sense. As relevant categories emerge and cannot be defined in a simple way, the study of architecture has to join hands with the science of complexity (again).[16]

Neapolitan nativity scene, Bavarian National Museum collection, Munich. Three-dimensional parallel worlds look back on a long tradition here.
The relevant market place is in the Via San Gregorio Armeno in Naples. Whereas many only play at trading in the Nativity, a few people can actually make a living from it.

Including Room 16, Villa dei Misteri, Pompeii. In the 1st century AD, artificial architecture extended reality in the Villa dei Misteri.

Archigram: collage, gallery project for Bournemouth, 1968, Archigram/Ron Herron.

Gilles Deleuze, Félix Guattari: *Tausend Plateaus*, Berlin 1992, S. 668:
*"You can live wedged into deserts,
steppes or oceans;
you can even live fluidly in cities,
and be an urban nomad."*

Throughout the ages, there have been other document conventions representing Utopias:
There are endless shopping opportunities for your
personal version of Utopia!

A man snowboards
with a "snowboard
simulator" in Sello
Shopping Center,
Espoo, Finland, 2007

Title page woodcut
from Sir Thomas
More's *Utopia*,
1516. The drawing
illustrates More's
idea of localizing
his ideal state on
an island over the
horizon in some part
of the New World.

40

No Place like Utopia
by *Steffen Krämer*

A nalogies are constantly being drawn – indeed, in this book as well – between Second Life and concepts of Utopia, which have existed since classical antiquity and acquired a specific meaning during the Renaissance. The word Utopia combines the two Greek words "ou", for non-, and "topos", for place.[17] Therefore strictly speaking, it signifies a non-place or a nowhere. Whereas this meaning is hard to grasp, it points to the title of a literary text published in 1516 and written by the English jurist and lord chancellor Thomas More.[18] In his novel More describes the model of an ideal state and refers to the location, in which it's society had developed historically and supposedly still existed in the sixteenth century. The location is named Utopia. According to More's idea, Utopia was an island in the sea beyond the horizon, located somewhere in the New World close to an unspecified coast. As a consequence More´s *Utopia* became a symbol for unexplored territory in the Age of Discovery, shortly after Christopher Columbus found the Americas at the end of the fifteenth century.

As a setting for the development of an ideal state, the distant island was perfect, since it would be completely free of the millennia-old chains of ancient European traditions. On an island where Europeans had never set foot, alternative notions of the state or city could have developed in a natural way, so that More's *Utopia* was conceived not so much as a nowhere-land as an as-yet unknown place somewhere, which is only nowhere yet in this world.

Later exponents of Utopian novels would also borrow the Morean idea of an island for their works. One example is Sir Francis Bacon's *New Atlantis* of 1627, which places its island with an ideal state somewhere in the Pacific.[19] By the beginning of the twentieth century such still undiscovered islands that could serve as a topographical reference point for an Utopian state were of course no longer available. Authors therefore had to cast around for new autonomous locations. Written in 1907 and published in 1929, Russian writer Alexander Bogdanow's novel *Red Planet* set his vision of a state on the planet Mars.[20] Utopia was thus now an as-yet undiscovered space-island in the solar system.

Political or social visionary worlds in the cosmos with extra-terrestrial ideal states were thereafter a firm part of the established repertory of sci-fi literature. However, since the 1980s, they have become a rather antiquated notion, since the computer-generated world of artificial reality offers the infinite facets of "islands in the net", such as American writer Bruce Sterling described in his cyberpunk novel of that title of 1988.[21] Thus More's *Utopia* can now develop within the boundless expanses of cyberspace.[22] The current paradigm of an island with an ideal urban community in virtual reality is Second Life.

The urban arrangement of this 3D online world is based on the grid, i.e. a three-dimensional grid-space, which is subdivided into individual square "sims" each with an identical area. Thus what distinguishes the grid of Second Life is a rigorously orthogonal geometricisation. Though the structure given at the beginning can be expanded, it cannot be changed. This regular diagram is uniform in shape and permanent, and therefore claims timeless validity. And precisely this concept of perfect harmony plus absolute immutability also characterises the shape of the cities in More's *Utopia*.[23] There are fifty-four of them in all on More's island,

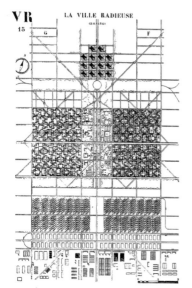

Le Corbusier: Ville Radieuse, early 1930s. An ideal city layout whose urban structure can be expanded at the sides but not basically changed.
The arrangement corresponds to a functional hierarchy.

Ludwig Hilberseimer: high-rise city, 1924. Anonymous figures indicated as dark silhouettes inhabit this anonymous urban vision. The artistic neutrality results almost inevitably in a loss of urban quality and individuality.

all with the identical urban structure, a square ground plan divided into four uniform districts and all buildings are the same distance from each other.

Utopian communities absolutely cry out for an ideal urban model, since they are held together in a perfect collective state that can tolerate change no more than it can imperfection. The city is thus the symbol of these communities, regardless of whether those of Utopia, New Atlantis or Second Life.

Meantime, what fundamentally distinguishes the Utopia of Second Life from its Renaissance and Baroque predecessors is the social structure of the ideal society. More and Bacon wrote their Utopian works seeking to combine their opposition to aspects of the set-up in their day with a quest for a better social order. In their view, Utopia would strive primarily for political or social perfection. Idealistic threads of this kind do not occur in Second Life. Though every user tries to perfect his virtual counterpart – the avatar – in its external appearance in accordance with his personal preferences, no intention of consolidating an urban collective is involved. On the contrary, an interesting and attractive external appearance increases the individual's chances of asserting his or her claims in the virtual beauty competition.

Moreover, "there is in Second Life no more popular activity than shopping", as explicitly stated in the official handbook to the virtual world.[24] This urban Utopia is thus clearly based on a simple consumer ideology, which is in addition permanently being optimised. In Second Life, profit rules, and the so-called land barons determine the distribution of urban land by trading in the virtual building land.[25] Not surprisingly, Anshe Chung – currently the richest resident of Second Life – is a real-estate dealer who has built a trading empire step by step from the sale of virtual property.[26] It is not the Utopia of an ideal society that dominates here but the real currency of hard US dollars.

This ultimately capitalist notion is however not entirely foreign to the historical development of Utopian urban models. The famous *ville radieuse* – radiant city – designed by Swiss architect Le Corbusier in the early 1930s is an urban vision likewise based on mercantile principles. The upper area, as it were the intellectual head of the whole urban area, is a mighty administration and business centre containing a total of fourteen huge office buildings in which an almost boundless mass of employees has to represent the values of a modern business world unconditionally. Like the city in Second Life, the *ville radieuse* is subdivided into geometrical plots, and again, this regular arrangement can be expanded laterally but not changed fundamentally. In contrast, Ludwig Hilberseimer's high-rise city of 1924 visualises indistinguishable rows of buildings in which the anonymous office-workers have to live. Loosely dispersed throughout the perspective representation of urban space their dark, stereotype figures are reminiscent of the avatars in Second Life. Though the latter are more colourful and more innovative, they look just as artificial. The urban scene in Hilberseimer's vertical city seems just as thinly populated as Second Life.

And finally, Second Life offers the countless facets of artificial backdrops in the various virtual urban areas. Sometimes they can be as obscure as Terry Gilliam's dystopian sci-fi vision in the film *Brazil*, which came out programmatically in 1984; sometimes they can be as happy and naïve as the architectonic scenery of Disneyland. Yet despite this at-first-glance astonishing richness of imaginative design, a quality of diagrammatic regularity always remains present in Second Life. No doubt this is due to the fact that every object, however complex, is constructed from a very limited stock of primary geometric shapes. These shapes

Still from *Brazil*, UK 1984. George Orwell
says in *1984*:
"The reality was decaying, dingy cities
where underfed people shuffled to
and fro in leaky shoes."

Utopia, an island in the sea...

Disneyland near
Los Angeles,
from the 1950s.
Breezy backdrops
from the
lowlands of trivial
architecture,
which attempt
to satisfy the
sentimental
desire for dream
fantasies in fairy-
tale glamour.

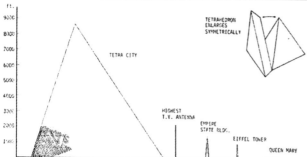

We find that a tetrahedronal city, to house a million people, is both technologically and economically feasible. Such a vertical-tetrahedronal-city can be constructed with all of its three hundred thousand families each having balconied "outside" apartments of two thousand square feet floor space. All of the machinery necessary to its operation will be housed inside the tetrahedron. It is found that such a one million passenger tetrahedronal city is so structurally efficient, and therefore so relatively light, that together with its hollow box sectioned reinforced concrete foundations it can float. Such tetrahedronal floating cities would measure two miles to an edge, and can be floated in a triangularly patterned canal. This will make the whole structure earthquake-proof. The whole city can be floated out into the ocean to any point and anchored. The depth of its foundations will go below the turbulence level of the seas so that the floating tetrahedronal island will be, in effect, a floating triangular atoll. Its two mile long "boat" foundations will constitute landing strips for jet airplanes. Its interior two mile harbor will provide refuge for the largest and smallest ocean vessels. The total structural and mechanical materials involved in production of a

number of such cities are within feasibility magnitude of the already operating metals manufacturing capabilities of any one company of the several major industrial nations around the earth. The tetrahedron city may start with a thousand occupants and grow symmetrically to hold millions without changing overall shape though always providing each family with 200 sq. ft. of floor space. Withdrawal of materials from obsolete buildings on the land will permit the production of enough of these floating cities to support frequently spaced floating cities of various sizes around the oceans of the earth. This will permit mid-ocean cargo transferring and therewith an extraordinary increase of efficiency of the inter-distribution of the world's raw and finished products as well as of the passenger traffic. Three quarters of the earth is covered by water. Man is clearly intent on penetrating those world-around ocean waters in every way to work both their ocean bottoms and their marine life and chemistry resources. Such ocean passage shortening habitats of ever transient humanity will permit his individual flying sailing, economic stepping stone travel around the whole Earth in many directions.

R. Buckminster Fuller. Three Utopian Projects: Tetrahedron City, late 1960s. The artificial island floats in San Francisco Bay atop Alcatraz, the high-security prison island from which nobody could escape.

form a monolithic dataset, in which every distinct bit is identified by a 16-byte character string. Just like with *The Matrix* in the 1999 sci-fi film by Larry and Andy Wachowski, it is hard to translate this dataset of endless alphabetical and digital codes into realistic virtual imagery. As a consequence we are still left with an abstract impression of cybernetic illusion. Second Life is definitely not as alive as reality.

There is nonetheless a complex urban vision to Second Life, and currently millions of people immerse themselves into it regularly. Yet it does not attain the degree of collective perfection, on a political, social or cultural level, that Thomas More attributed to his classic model in the early sixteenth century. So it is quite in order to borrow a phrase from that well-known doyen of American architectural criticism Peter Blake, who named his late-twentieth century personal memoirs *No Place like Utopia*.[27]

Morpheus: *"The matrix is omnipresent. It surrounds us, you can feel it. ... It is an illusionary world you foster so as to keep at bay the truth that you are a slave."*
QUOTED FROM THE FILM "MATRIX", USA 1999

ENDNOTES:
1 GOMBRICH 1979, P. 210; ON THE EYE AS A HIEROGLYPH FOR GOD SEE BREDEKAMP 1994, ESP. P. 298, FIG. 3; ON CORBUSIER'S OPEN HAND SEE AMONG OTHERS LE CORBUSIER 1960, P. 278, AND LE CORBUSIER JEANNERET 1957–65, VOL. 7, P. 109, BOTTOM RIGHT.

2 SEE SL HANDBOOK 2007, P. V; FOR THE MORALLY MOTIVATED RESEARCHER IT MIGHT BE ADDED, THAT MAJOR PARTS OF THE HISTORY OF ART NEED TO BE EXCLUDED IF WE CONSIDER OUR SUBJECTS ACCORDING TO THE MORAL INTEGRITY OF THEIR PROTAGONISTS.

3 OTHER EXAMPLES OF SUCH 3D SPACES INCLUDE THERE, WORLD OF WAR CRAFT AND IN SOME RESPECTS ALSO GOOGLE EARTH; IMPORTANT TERMS IN THIS CIRCUMSTANCE ARE "METAVERSE" AND "MASSIVELY MULTIPLAYER ONLINE ROLE-PLAYING GAME". SEE THE CORRESPONDING WIKIPEDIA ENTRIES FOR EACH.

4 ON LOCAL ACTIVITY AS A FOUNDATION OF COMPLEXITY SEE CHUA 2005; ON COMPLEXITY IN GENERAL SEE ÉRDI 2008.

5 SEE FOR EXAMPLE ECONOMIST 2007 ON THE NECESSARY REGULATION OF THE SECOND LIFE MONETARY MARKET.

6 INTERESTINGLY THE OFFICIAL DOCUMENTATION OF THE INFRASTRUCTURE (SEE HTTP://SECONDLIFEGRID.NET) DOES NOT STATE, IF "SECOND LIFE GRID" MEANS THE REPRESENTED SPACE GRID OR A GRID OF SERVERS IN THE SENSE OF GRID-COMPUTING. IN FACT THE INFRASTRUCTURE CONSISTS OF A LOCAL GROUP OF COMPUTERS WHICH ARE NOT DISTRIBUTED ARBITRARILY; SEE IN DETAIL WIKIPEDIA ENTRIES FOR "COMPUTER CLUSTER" AND "GRID COMPUTING".

7 FOR AN INTRODUCTION ON THE SL GRID, SIMS, PRIMS AND AVATARS SEE SL HANDBOOK 2007 PP. 10, 12, 132FF AND 146–148.

8 SEE BETTENCOURT, ET AL 2007.

9 FOR THE DEFINITION OF METAOPTICAL SEE SUMMERS 2003, P. 555FF AND P. 685; ON THE ORIGINS OF OUR MODERN NOTION OF GRID-SPACE SEE PEHNT 1983.

10 AN IMPORTANT STEP HEREBY WOULD BE THE DECOUPLING OF THE INFRASTRUCTURE FROM THE SPACE GRID, FOR E.G. WITH A DISTRIBUTED COMPUTING-GRID, WHERE MULTIPLE COMPUTERS ADD TO THE DENSITY OF A SINGLE SQUARE OF AREA; SEE WIKIPEDIA ENTRY FOR "GRID COMPUTING".

11 SEE SL HANDBOOK 2007 P. 132FF; FOR THE NOTATION OF PLANTS SEE SECOND LIFE WIKI ENTRY "CUSTOM LINDEN PLANTS".

12 ON "UNIVERSAL UNIQUE IDENTIFIERS" (UUID) SEE SL HANDBOOK 2007, P. 9.

13 THE SUBJECTIVITY OF DIVISION OF REAL OBJECTS AND PROBLEMS COMING WITH IT BECOME EVIDENT BY COMPARING HIERARCHICAL DESCRIPTIONS OF HISTORIC MONUMENTS AND DOCUMENTS; SEE SCHICH 2007 PP. 34–46.

14 THE OBSERVATIONS ON JOHN CONSTABLE'S PAINTING OF WIVENHOE PARK IN GOMBRICH 1960 SEEM RELEVANT IN THIS CIRCUMSTANCE.

15 RECOGNIZING THE DIFFERENCE IS LEARNABLE: SEE ELKINS 2000, PP. 108–117.

16 THE STUDY OF ARCHITECTURE AND NETWORKS AS COMPLEX PHENOMENA JOINED A LONG TIME AGO: SEE WIGLEY 2001; FOR A HISTORY OF SOCIAL NETWORK ANALYSIS SEE FREEMAN 2004; ON COMPLEX NETWORKS IN GENERAL SEE BARBÁSI 2002.

17 ON THE ETYMOLOGIC ROOTS OF THE WORD UTOPIA SEE SAAGE 1991, P. 2.

18 THOMAS MORE'S NOVEL UTOPIA OF 1516 IS REPRINTED IN: DER UTOPISCHE STAAT 1960, PP. 7–110. ALL RELEVANT INFORMATION IS TAKEN FROM THIS GERMAN TRANSLATION.

19 FRANCIS BACON'S NEW ATLANTIS OF 1627 IS REPRINTED IN GERMAN TRANSLATION IN: DER UTOPISCHE STAAT 1960, PP. 171–215.

20 BOGDANOV 1989, PP. 5–154.

21 STERLING 1988.

22 THE TERM CYBERSPACE FOR A COMPUTER-SIMULATED ARTIFICIAL REALITY WAS COINED BY THE AMERICAN AUTHOR WILLIAM GIBSON IN HIS 1984 NOVEL NEUROMANCER; SEE GIBSON 2005, P. 87.

23 ON THE CONFIGURATION OF CITIES IN THOMAS MORE'S UTOPIA SEE DER UTOPISCHE STAAT 1960, PP. 49–53 AND 59FF.

24 SL HANDBOOK 2007, P. 63.

25 FOR LAND BARONS AND VIRTUAL LAND IN SECOND LIFE SEE SL HANDBOOK 2007 PP. 37–39, 283, AND MÜLLER 2007, P. 154.

26 ON ANSHE CHUNG SEE SL HANDBOOK 2007, P. 214 AND 251, AND SPIEGEL 2007, P. 151, 153.

27 BLAKE 1996.

BIBLIOGRAPHY: SEE PAGE 156

VIRTUALIZATION

– MARIO GEROSA

Some surreal landscapes in two postcards of the beginning of the 20th century. The cities are hybridated with icons of a possible future and they look like video game sets. In other postcards, a medical metaphysical space forebodes the dark corridors of *Silent Hill*.

It's easy to say virtual. In particular, when talking about virtual architecture, people fail to refine enough, to take account of all kinds of nuances and typologies that include for example imaginary architecture, ephemeral architecture, virtual architecture in fantasy novels, virtual architecture of synthetic universes, ephemeral architecture reflecting the architecture of reality, vanished virtual architecture of synthetic worlds and architecture we have wondrous accounts of but in fact never existed. In a word, there are degrees of distinction between virtual and real, a spectrum of almost infinite variants, or if you prefer, a large number of degrees of virtualization.

And you don't have to think immediately of synthetic worlds and video games. There's no need to speak of virtual worlds in networks to refer to virtual architecture. Thousands of gradations between the real and the imaginary have always existed, in speech, books, actors' gestures and the taradiddles of those who lie to take people in or colour a story. Virtuality was not invented yesterday. It goes back thousands of years, accompanying man like a shadow ever since the beginning of time. In the case of architecture, it applies to the middle-class houses of Alberto Savinio, Arnold Bennett's Grand Babylon Hotel or Enigma House in Anarchy Online. There are various degrees of virtualization, meaning by this term the capacity of architecture and the landscape to shift from an unambiguous model into an open organism instead, capable of offering various intertextual approaches.

The first degree of virtualization concerns fragmented landscapes. To create exploded landscapes is the first step towards realising landscapes designed as open structures, as "landscapes in progress". In fact, here we are still at a base level inasmuch as it is solely a question of demonstrating that such architectures are not closed and hermetic. Experiments of this type have been carried out for example by David Hockney, who has produced exploded visions in which the landscape tends to break up, which adopt as it were the physiognomy of a cloud, thanks to a series of chemo-emotional reactions. Features emerge that were not visible while the landscape and the architecture were solid.

An imaginary vision: the sea in Piazza del Duomo in Milan. The postcards were a strong medium for the pre-virtuality. On the A side there were visions of curious places and situations. On the B side there was the description of someone who gave a personal interpretation of that landscape. This way, the virtuality increased.

"This Grand Hotel de Balbec was perhaps not like the sole stage set in certain provincial theatres where a wide range of compositions were put on, that was used for a comedy, a first tragedy, a second or a purely poetic drama."

– Marcel Proust,
The Fugitive

Three early screenshots of *Second Life*. These structures belong to the first period of the history of the virtual world by Linden Lab. These early icons prove that we can provide a historicisation of synthetic worlds.

A screenshot from *Myst IV Revelation*. In the saga of *Myst* Robyn and Rand Miller created a complete surreal environment: it was a big achievement in the direction of the virtualization of spaces. Those adventure games also implied the birth of a new discipline, tourism in video games, a practice that would have been very requested in the golden age of virtual worlds.

At the moment when the reaction takes place, besides the elements of classic landscape iconography – previously lost in the general setting – adrenaline and passions emerge, and a sense of the sublime and the like help to establish an emotional landscape. You switch from the standard landscape to the emotional landscape. And even here there is already a certain sense of virtuality, intended as an extra feature inherent in the landscape and the architecture.

A sense of virtuality is found in the Romantic landscapes of Constable and Turner and the visionary landscapes of Caspar David Friedrich or in certain settings of *Guild Wars* and *Star Wars Galaxies*. It is exactly the same virtuality, but worked out in different ways. As observed earlier, the fragmentation and discombobulation of the landscape set up a reaction of chemical origin that releases the various essential components. To make this clear, let us take as an example videogames such as *Doom 3* and *Silent Hill*. Despite appearances, because the mix of dark architecture, laboratories, rooms barred with chains and bolts, gloomy corridors and spaceships from the hereafter, these landscapes are formed of the adrenaline of those who visit and traverse them. The adrenaline is not simply a glue but a fundamental constituent. When this adrenaline is released, it manifests the character of virtuality typical of scary settings like these.

But there are many other types of virtualization, and to go into the matter in detail we need to take a closer look at the nature of imaginary architecture, which may fall into various typologies according to the following categories: totally fictitious places, hybrid places and places similar to real ones.

IN TOTALLY FICTIONAL PLACES:

36,9 * Few elements are given;

37,0 * there are no references to examples already known;

37,1 * sometimes it is difficult to imagine successfully transporting these places into real life.

37,2 * Totally imaginary places are less self-referential.

37,3 * Fictitious places are the heritage of everyone.
In a certain sense, they are "open source architecture".

37,4 * In fictitious places, communication is mainly of a psychological nature.

37,5 * Communication of an emotion, a mode of perceiving the architecture.

37,6 * The handling of architecture in literature tends to exclude references to real life

37,7 * Archetypal typologies are suggested (e.g. labyrinthine forms)

37,8 * Few references

37,9 * Architecture of sensations

38,0 * "Liquid" space

38,1 * Scary architecture, which is communicated by:

– *highlighting the more disturbing aspects (theories of staircases that lead to nothing, closed doors, dungeons, attics)*
– *creating a synaesthesia between people and architecture.*
– *favouring movement (to communicate unease, I have to imagine that an architecture or a place is being traversed). In fact, potentially dynamic places are more dangerous than static ones (scary tunnels, responsive architecture, levels of video games).*

WHEREAS, AS REGARDS HYBRID PLACES...

They are distinct in being the result of a cross-pollination of RL and fantasy; such cross-pollinations are often well concealed; not infrequently, they are places inspired by settings linked to the lives of those who describe them.

Hybrid places are easily reinterpreted and shared. Anyone can make use of such architectures with a degree of freedom. There is a framework – a defined structure – to which a host of variations can be added. To get these places across, I have to distil an idea of common experience that everyone can share.

Thus the message is twofold: I communicate on the one hand an imaginary place; on the other the real part contained in the fictitious place.

38,2 * An example of a hybrid space is the Grand Hotel de Balbec, in Proust's *Recherche*, an architecture that sets up self-referential communication.
38,3 * Imaginary part: Theatre, church, grand hotel, casino, baths...
38,4 * Part based on real life: large fin-de-siècle hotel in a Norman spa resort...

For places similar to real ones, it is not necessary to carry out a close examination. It seems more interesting to note instead how such places can be re-interpreted by applying an architectural rhetoric that could for example use figures of speech such as:

  – *oxymoron (contrasting terms – lucid folly, hotel prison)*
  – *hyperbole (seven-star hotel, hyperrealist places like certain theme restaurants)*
  – *paradox (Las Vegas Venice)*
  – *metaphor (essence of places)*

At this stage, we have defined the fundamental elements of the syntax of imaginary and virtual architecture. But to get a clearer idea of the immenseness of the subject, pending an adequate classification, it is useful to allude to other important examples. One of the first possibilities concerns illustrated postcards of landscapes. Here the architecture is two-sided – it can be read in two different ways. I can look at it on side A, the one with the picture, and

A screenshot of a landscape of *Sinking Island*, the latest video game by Benoit Sokal. In the video games conceived by this French author the architecture is always mutable and mysterious, like the university of *Barockstadt* in *Syberia*.
© BLE

STYLES OF VIRTUALIZATION

Necessary misunderstandings between virtual styles vs. so-called real (physical) architecture...

1 * **ESOTERIC STEAMPUNK**
VR: Myst, Riven, Uru, Schizm

Corresponding style in reality:
Gothic style.

2 * **CLASSIC STEAMPUNK**
Project Nomads.

Corresponding style in reality:
Neo-Classic

3 * **LUDIC SURREALISM**
American MgGee Alice

Corresponding style in reality:
German expressionistic architecture
(Mendelsohn, Hugo Häring,
Bruno Taut).

Above: a screenshot from **Project Entropia**,
now **Entropia Universe**. © MINDARK
Right: an artwork from Richard Garriott's
Tabula Rasa recalls the style of Turner. © CSOFT

In the video game *Portal* the virtualization of space reaches the highest degree. Here the player must create brand-new spaces as he walks and explores. But he also needs to solve very difficult architectural puzzles, as if he were in an upgraded Escher world. *Portal* concentrates in itself all the specifics of a tour in a virtualized space: the emotional walk full of pain, the creative travel where one has to interpret spaces and the sense to finish in the middle of nowhere.
© Valve/Electronic Arts

there I will have an appropriate view of the countryside. I see it the way thousands of other recipients of such cards can see it. Or I can analyse it on side B, the one on which people write addresses and comments. And then I have a kind of subtitle to the landscape, a caption provided by the unconscious that can offer suggestions about the way to enjoy this place. In that case, the virtualization lies precisely between the two sides of the card, and is expressed the moment the card is turned over and the illustrated part gives way to the written part.

There are then even more sophisticated ways of virtualising the landscape – for example, those concerning the body. The alchemy between the body and the landscape is complex, and traditionally includes numerous links and relationships. The anatomy of the body has various terms that relate to the landscape (ranging from the "mons Veneris" to the "Island of Reil" (insular cortex) and the "promontory" of the spinal column), and likewise many artists have indulged in anthropomorphising the landscape.

Generally speaking, bodies and landscapes are seen as two elements that need to be kept separate. In the fragmented landscapes of David Hockney the viewer is essential in order to define the existence of the landscape, perceived as the other, and the same happens in first-person shooters (FPS), as also in *Quake* and *Doom*, where a gaze in a subjective shot is there to justify the setting being passed through. Thus bodies and landscapes traditionally cannot coincide. It is one thing to say that the landscape is filled with emotion, but something else again to assert that the container in which those emotions are flowing can also adhere to the scenery seen. Now, this is a point that Chinese artist Huang Yan has turned upside down, photographing bodies with landscapes tattooed on them. It is an important change for virtualization, indeed it means going beyond the barrier between bodies and landscapes, short-circuiting the concept of distance between the viewer and the place.

The idea of distance is constantly being put up for discussion in this discourse and is central to the analysis of the various grades of virtualization. For example, the coordinates of distance are forever being rendered nugatory in virtual worlds that use teleporting. The idea of traversed space and effort is nullified here, as a result of which any idea of an encounter in front of a given monument ceases to exist, and the idea of waiting also loses its meaning. In *Second Life*, for example, I can teleport an avatar near me so my body becomes itself the place of the meeting. There's no need to have a physical location – the body expands conceptually and becomes the meeting point. It is a body that incorporates the landscape ideally, and conversely records the tattooed drawings of Huang Yan.

As was said earlier, this discourse unhinges the concept of time, given that waiting is reduced to a minimum. Such virtualization tends to simplify time and space, eliminating the superfluous, early arrivals and delays. In the same fashion but in a way more bound up with space, new satellite systems eliminate the superfluous. Given an opportunity, space is removed, unexpectedly, at the risk of making a mistake. Journeys become linear, time no longer being wasted on possible deviations, it's straight to the point without any digressions. This removes a wide margin from virtualization conceived as a neutral space of indecisiveness and the unforeseen. Thus, paradoxically, virtual worlds, in which there should be maximum space for virtualization understood as neutral territory for free interpretation, become places where meanings are more clear-cut, where places no longer lend themselves to possible misunderstandings. In particular, journeys heading towards places become unambiguous, eliminating the practice of wandering around and moving without purpose. In virtual worlds, the tendency is to proceed straight off.

So, does that really mean that virtuality is on the way out in terms of the indefinite potential for choice? Not exactly. In fact, virtual architecture is intentionally full of fractures and gaps left precisely to encourage the practice of virtualization. The virtual architectures of Second Life are based on a deliberate ambiguity, miles away from the certitudes of architecture in the real world. Moreover, they are architectures that elude any kind of pre-existent parameters. If you think of the palaces, emporia, blockhouses, factories, skyscrapers and hospitals in MMORPGs (Massive Multiplayer Online Role-playing Games), you note that there are almost always more or less concealed references to the aesthetics of the real world. The references are however rather evanescent and oblique, reconstructing and reinventing styles, making the definition of new aesthetic criteria necessary. I considered this problem some time ago, seeking to define a series of styles.
(See right column "Styles of Virtualization", pp. 49 – 50)

As may be guessed, making reference to the schemes outlined at the beginning, we still find ourselves in a phase of transition. We are looking at hybrid places that are not yet liberated from references to the history of architecture. In reality, in Second Life this whole system of references is more precarious. We are unable to distinguish precise trends, movements and stylistic tendencies. Thus there is more room for interpretation and virtualization. Everyone can project on the architecture what s/he sees or wants to see. Ultimately in Second Life, language blueprints are also being established, a tendency to read in two different modes. We find on the one hand architectures similar to the installations of Jenny Holzer or Barbara Kruger, on the other, reactive architectures that create words and phrases on visitor contact.

Reported architecture can also develop. In virtual worlds like Second Life, the architecture is liable to vanish. People pay rent to build on a sim and sometimes decide to abandon it, leaving everything that has been built to disappear. Similarly, spaces are defined that exist solely by virtue of the temporary presence of groups of people. Spaces are created and disappear by virtue of aggregations of groups, rather like raves and flash mobs in the real world. In this sense, the level of virtualization is considerably augmented. In fact, the spaces become really immaterial and can actually turn out as cases of architecture conceived as metropolitan

S P A C E

4. **POST-ATOMIC FUNCTIONALSM**
Duke Nukem, Half-Life, Doom, Quake, Marathon

Corresponding style in reality: Contemporary avantgarde architecture: Will Alsop, Nox, Zaha Hadid, Frank Gehry, Graft...

5. **NEODRAMATIC**
Silent Hill, Resident Evil, Project Zero, Haunting Ground, Forbidden Siren.

Victorian Style, Edwardian Style, "Eward-Hopperian"- Style

6. **FANTASY**
Lineage, World of Warcraft, Guild Wars, EverQuest.

Theme Parks, medival cities, Jerde,

7. **POST DÉCO**
City of Heroes, City of Villains.

Las Vegas.

8. **LUDIC VIRTUAL SURREALISM**
Second Life, The Sims Online, Sociolotron, There.

Antoni Gaudi, Hundertwasser, Blob architecture.

9. **FUTURE GLAM**
Entropia Universe, Anarchy Online.

Novosibirsk, Buddha Bar.

10. **ABSTRACT DECO**
Habbo Hotel.

Richard Meier, Toio Ito, Mendini, Ettore Sottsass, Legoland.

11. **TECHNO-DYNAMIC LANDSCAPES**
Need for Speed, Sim City, Grand Theft Auto.

Shanghai, Dubai, OMA.

legends. At this stage, it can happen that you talk of virtual architecture that really existed but then vanished, handed down in accounts of those who saw it, or else you can talk of architecture that was said to have existed but in reality was never realised. In this sense, we are in the presence of a squared virtual, given that what we are offered are descriptions of imaginary places linked to a virtual universe. It is an update of the inventions of writers who conceive imaginary architecture – except that when fantasy places connected with books are mentioned, you are biased – you know that those places do not exist and never have existed.

But if I speak of a fantasy place that could or ought to have existed in a synthetic world like Second Life, doubt remains. In every respect, this involves the suspension of disbelief, and it is more than legitimate to think that such ephemeral architectures might have existed. We are also in the zone of probability. Thus, if people say to me that a virtual architecture with the features of the Grand Hotel de Balbec from Proust's Recherche existed in Second Life, it is legitimate for me to believe it. It is a question of a reference that is difficult to verify but which seems absolutely plausible. It is a virtualization carried to extremes that has the benefit of doubt and is difficult to refute. For this reason as well, it appears useful to think of a form of classification or archiving of our legacy of virtual architecture. In this way, with a census of the ephemeral products of synthetic universes, it would avoid the risk of a rather forced ambiguity and could guarantee a precise picture of how much has been achieved in virtual worlds over the years.

The Convention for the preservation of our heritage of virtual architecture, which I launched in June 2006, is a response to these requirements and is based on the Convention for the preservation of the architectural heritage of Europe drawn up in Granada in 1985.

Here is what the document says:

ARTICLE 1
The Purpose of this Convention

1.1

Since the Renaissance there has been a strong desire for ideal cities and imaginary architecture. They often were idealistic and utopian visions that traced new directions for architecture. Some were avant-garde architectural projects, while others reflected the social aspirations of a particular culture. From the painting of *La città ideale* in the Urbino Palazzo Ducale to the drawings of Lequeu and Sant'Elia, these paper and canvas representations of architecture tell us a great deal about a historical period.

Now there is a new form of ideal architecture, that of video games, either single player or multiplayer networked video games. This architecture is not physical and indeed is immaterial but these constructions are not completely imaginary, as they can be considered a form of architectural drawings. In a certain sense, they exist as real architecture, but not on a normal physical plane. They exist only inside the computers that run them, and the storage media that contain their data. In particular, in the last decade many new synthetic worlds have been born, the so-called MMOGs (Massively Multiplayer Online Games) and MMORPGs (Massively Multiplayer Online Role-playing Games). In these new worlds one can find many new forms of architecture. Some are based on designs that recall the architectural forms of real life, there are also worlds of a wholly original style. For this reason, they are original and evolutionary expressions of art and must be preserved. In fact, in these worlds there is an intense and chaotic urban development, largely uncontrolled by any form of authority, and there is the risk that architecture and environments created to populate these worlds will disappear and be lost forever.

At first glance, the architecture of synthetic worlds is more abstract than the paper blueprints and representations of traditional architecture, but in fact they are just as real, because people live in and interact with these constructs just as they do in the real world, though in a manner reflecting the differences between real-world and synthetic-world.

Traditional drawings and representations of imaginary architecture are not inhabited, and thus are static beyond changes that the original designer may make. The virtual architecture of video games, particularly MMOGs, either are or have the potential to be constantly evolving. The architecture of single player games is also dependent on the people who play them and subject to modification and addition by these same players.

Here is a crucial point: some will say that we don't need a convention for the protection of the virtual architectural heritage, because the videogames are already collected by some institutions that keep a copy of every video game published, as for the movies, etc. There is, however, a strong difference: here we don't refer to the video game itself as a whole creative product, but to the architecture and environments contained within the video games, believing that they represent valid and new aesthetical forms that reflect the spirit of our time and that they are also an example of the new directions taken by contemporary architecture. All this theory will result clearer in the next future, when (at least is believable), famous architects will begin to create projects for video games. When outstanding architects will begin to create video game architecture, they will gain a different reputation and also the already existing "in game" architectures will increase their value.

1.2

A central concept for the architecture of video games is that they are part of the action. They live together with the characters. They are often theatrical architecture, with traps, moving walls, pitfalls, etc. They respond to every move of the player: in that way, they are living, organic creatures. But they also live because they are visited, admired and interacted with by people.

A number of base considerations emerge from the document. In the first place, there is a need to define the quality of such architecture, which is very distinct from that of the real world. For this, it will be necessary to define an appropriate aesthetic canon, with new styles. And if, as has been said, these days it is no longer possible to talk of styles, it is legitimate to think of creating provisional categories for the purpose of starting a dialogue, constructing a common grammar and syntax. Then, once the parameters for assessing the best architecture

Sim City, 2007. © Electronic Arts

"Around the time I began to think about the concept for the Sims, our
house burnt down to the foundation walls.
We had nothing left and had to start from scratch.
Buy a house, clothes, toothbrush, car, just about everything.
I found it exciting to see how and in what order we rebuilt our lives.
And that's just what the Sims is about.
When you play, you build a life out of nothing."

— WILL WRIGHT

(ORIGINAL DESIGNER OF POPULAR COMPUTER GAMES SUCH AS SIMCITY, THE SIMS AND NOW SPORE)

have been firmed up, these provisional labels can be discarded. The other thread concerns the concept of participatory architecture, which exists solely by virtue of the presence of people using it. This is the most interesting architecture in Second Life, a nomad world in motion in which the most intriguing places are the non-places that elude the idea of barycentres, plazas and a monumental presence. And the very concept of plazas, which in Second Life are avoided and seen in negative, with all the outlines turned upside down, is a case in point of the idea of imaginary places in the virtual worlds, an example of the maximum degree of virtualization that can be achieved. And now, by way of summarising, a <u>decalogue</u> to define the "negative plazas" of Second Life.

1- *In Second Life there are no plazas with a symbolic value.*
   In real life (RL) there are statues that extol famous people of the past.

2- *In Second Life, there is no cult of the past and thus there*
   are no plazas with celebratory value.

3 - *Second Life is a dynamic world.*

4 - *Plazas tend to centralise.*

5 - *Second Life is a fluid universe of liquid architecture.*

6 - *The sole classic plazas of Second Life are those replicating the real*
   world that become mementos. Like the "snowballs", they are "in vitro places".

7 - *Plazas in RL are justified by a palace, church or market.*
   In Second Life, there is no focus on typological architecture of that kind.

8 - *Plazas represent moments of stopping. In virtual worlds,*
   life goes on like on a non-stop conveyor belt.

9 - *Often the plazas in real life (RL) are connected to representations of power that*
   presuppose that crowds will gather there. In Second Life there are no crowds.
   It's a lot if there are fifty people there.

Second Life is experienced as a holiday. And when you're on holiday, you don't go to the plaza but to the sea front or a disco instead. The plaza is for the natives.
Second Life does not have a historic centre and does not include the classic notion of squares. Plazas are bound up with the spatial representation of a community, and in Second Life it is rare to feel you are part of a single community.

The tenth point remains blank. Deliberately. Because plazas traditionally identify a barycentre, possibly among the palaces that identify the various powers present in that place. But the problem is that in Second Life, as in other virtual worlds, the barycentre has been moved outside the synthetic space and is outside, beyond the screen. So it is superfluous to try to define virtual plazas or architectural elements by poking among the prims or peeping among the ephemeral palaces of the synthetic universes, given that to understand how such architectural elements function you need to look within the screen while keeping sight of real life out of the corner of your eye.

See Mario Gerosa, "Turisti per gioco. Il viaggio nei videogame", in: Storia del turismo. Annale 2004, ed. Annunziata Berrino, Milan 2005.
Mario Gerosa, "Ludico, ionico, corinzio. Arte e architettura nei mondi virtuali", in: Virtual Geographic. Viaggi nei mondi dei videogiochi, ed. Ivan Fulco, Milan 2006.
http://virtualarchitecturalheritage.blogspot.com/2006/09/text-of-convention.
http://virtualarchitecturalheritage.blogspot.com/2006/09/text-of-convention.html

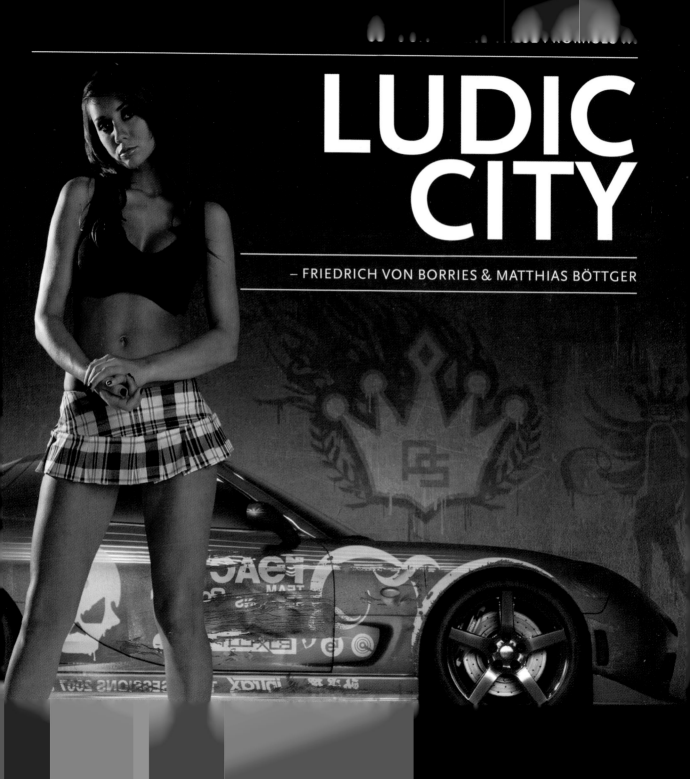

LUDIC CITY

– FRIEDRICH VON BORRIES & MATTHIAS BÖTTGER

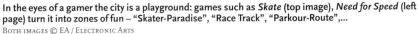

In the eyes of a gamer the city is a playground: games such as *Skate* (top image), *Need for Speed* (left page) turn it into zones of fun – "Skater-Paradise", "Race Track", "Parkour-Route",...
BOTH IMAGES © EA / ELECTRONIC ARTS

COMPUTER GAMES, SPACE AND ARCHITECTURE

People prospect for gold on "gold farms" – virtual gold, but panned with real sweat. In China, small software companies offering a special type of service are called gold firms. For 24 hours the staff plays multi-user dungeons (MUDs) such as *World of Warcraft* and other games where gamers have to laboriously build up the particular capabilities, strengths and characteristics of their avatars. Gold and guest workers from China speed things up. Either the accelerated avatars are directly commissioned or are developed for stock and then auctioned on eBay. Gamers from the rich "first" world can thus avoid the laborious work of constructing avatars. This is how the geographical and economic relationships of the globalised world are reflected in computer games as well, or to be more precise, in the virtual world that opens up between people as a result of a computer game.

There is a wholly different relationship between space and people in *Colossal Cave Adventure*, one of the earliest computer games, developed by William Crowther[1] in 1975/76. When his marriage was breaking up, programmer and speleologist Crowther wrote a computer game to entertain his children, although he was nowhere near at hand. The topographical antecedent and source of his game was the Mammoth Cave, a legendary cave system in

When gaming becomes a job: earning real dollars in so-called "Goldfarms" with virtual weapons and tools for Multi-user-dungeons games such as *World of Warcraft*.
WWW.CHINESEGOLDFARMERS.COM

The text-adventure game
Collosal Cave blends with
physical space.

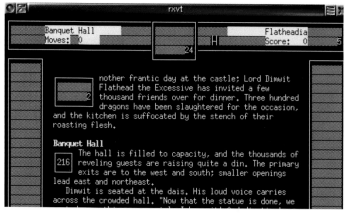

Parkour is an art to help you
overcome any obstacle to go from
point A to point B only with the
human body´s possibilities.

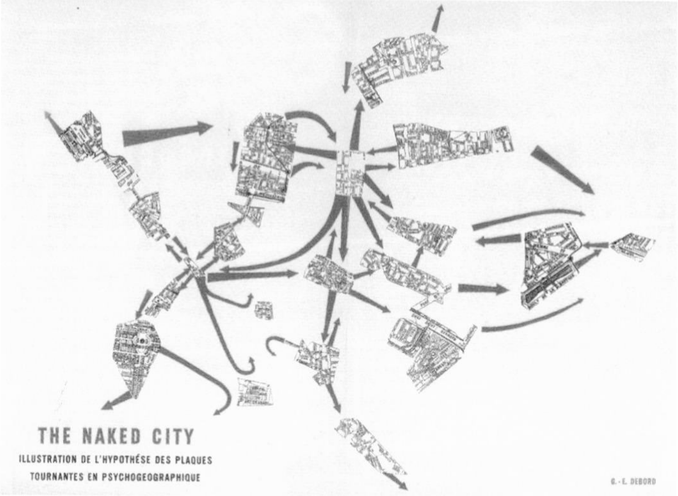

The Parkour runner´s ability to instant
map making calls to mind of Guy Debord
and the ideas of the Situationists such as
collecting the lost and found pieces of the
city by unplanned walks.
That process was called "Derivé".

THE NAKED CITY

ILLUSTRATION DE L'HYPOTHÈSE DES PLAQUES
TOURNANTES EN PSYCHOGEOGRAPHIQUE

G.-E. DEBORD

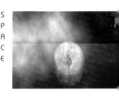

Kentucky.[2] In order to solve puzzles and overcome opponents, the player had to find his way through the cave. *Colossal Cave* is a text adventure, the spaces passed through being described in words. Navigating through space was effected by using commands "go west", "go south" etc. The spatial sense that developed thereby was so precise that practised players could orientate in the real cave on the basis of their in-game experiences.

As these two historically unconnected examples show, computer games are a highly spatial matter. And where there is space, architects are not far away. How space arises and how it achieves its effect is the basic issue of architecture. Good architecture involves not only the material shape of the built environment but also its effect on and interaction with users. It would thus seem a matter of course for architects to become interested in virtual spaces as well. Yet in reality most architects focus on what we know as physically built space. This is a limitation which one hopes will vanish in the near future, because the aesthetic and social qualities inherent in virtual spaces are a spatial challenge and opportunity. After all, it is architects who design the environment we live in. More and more commonly that includes not only the physical world but also virtual worlds. There too spaces develop that have real effects on our coexistence and actions.

Virtual spaces are projection surfaces for spatial ideas that are not realisable in the physical world. The different forms these may take are beautifully demonstrated in Second Life. The spectrum ranges from adapted, customised dreams of the middle classes with shopping centres and detached family homes to flight and projection fantasies of "another life", expressed architecturally in Yona Friedman's famous realisation of an architectural utopia, *Ville Spatiale*.[3]

Ville Spatial - a utopia in Second Life based on the vision of Yona Friedman, initiated by Stephan Lorenz.
HTTP://SLURL.COM/SECONDLIFE/ CULTUREGION/143/214/61

More interesting for architects than the transfer of architectural codes onto virtual worlds such as Second Life is the overlaying of the physical world with the virtual. That's because virtual space can be structurally informative for the physical world. This is particularly evident, visible and tangibly experienced in computer games, which in the course of their now thirty-year history have emerged from the screen and conquered real everyday space as "ubiquitous games". The setting is the city.

WHY THESE SPACES ARE A PROMISE ...

Botfighter, developed by Swedish company It's Alive several years ago, is a good example of such an overlay. The game is simple. Every player is a fighting robot. Fighting is by texting. Weapons, armour and other equipment can be bought on the Internet. You are in the game once you turn your mobile on, so the game breaches the barriers of space and time. The battle begins once another player enters the same radio cell. The whole battle game is a text adventure communicated via text messaging that takes place in the real physical world. In Stockholm, where the game was first tried out, players cycled through the city to get from cell to cell more quickly and find new opponents and adventures. Like all ubiquitous games, *Botfighter* promises a new, exciting playful city. In having such visions, ubiquitous games strikingly resemble the ideas of the Situationists. The artistic protest movement of the Situationists, who were active from the 1950s to the 1970s, demanded and designed a new city with lots happening. They developed methods, strategies and practices for conquering and implementing this city. Unplanned wandering about (the *dérive*) was seen as one new way to perceive and explore urban space. *Détournement* was another. Mobile and ubiquitous

Ubiquitous games such as Bofighter cross reality: Gaming with the mobile phone and SMS.
© IT'S ALIVE INC. 2002

games are nowadays adopting these concepts again, turning our everyday spatial experience inside out and getting us out and about in the city, thereby promising us a new urbanism in a new city. The environment we live in can thus be influenced not only by physical change (e.g. construction) but by immaterial changes as well (e.g. playing games).

... THAT REMAINS UNFULFILLED...

But this new generation of commercial games cannot fulfil the Situationist dream because they separate the idea of an adventurous city from its critical social context and transform it into a base for the consumption-oriented, fun-loving society. To misquote Adorno, "there is no true play in the false", because instead of a free, play-minded city, ubiquitous games generate a surveillance city. To play ubiquitously I leave my coordinates behind and reveal my pattern of movement and behavioural structures. One could almost believe games were a disguise for a new, now-voluntary form of control. It is not for nothing that "control" is a widely used term in the community. Almost all mobile online games can be interpreted as a voluntary introduction of surveillance, i.e. self-induced surveillance. Suspension of disbelief becomes the suspension of misbehaviour and resistance. In its future combat system, the US military employs standard games interfaces to control weapon systems so as to facilitate rapid learning and intuitive use.[4] No one can wage virtual war as well as someone who has done it since he had his first games console.

"Creative misuse" – a game that was not used as intended: the *Barcode Battler*.
© Epoch Co. Ltd. 1991

Thus in the media society playing could lead to people accepting voluntary dependency and spending time in more and more pre-set, controlled spaces. Or do games open up new possibilities for spatial interaction after all? For subversion, diversity and future?

... BUT NONETHELESS HAS SUBVERSIVE POTENTIAL

Wherever there is surveillance, there is always a way out as well – a trick. Creative misuse is the watchword that indicates a way out of the control dilemma in games. A good example of this is *Barcode Battler*, a Japanese game from the 1990s. The business idea behind the game was that players collected cards to read into the games console with a barcode reader. But many players wouldn't dream of spending money on these cards if there were much more exciting codes about everywhere. They went to the supermarket and used the games console to read in the bar codes of chewing gum packages etc. In this, the game and its technology became a tool of environmental exploration through creative misuse.

Play can also be an instrument of criticism and emancipation, as Jane McGonigal's game *Ministry of Reshelving* shows. It is a very simple, purely analogue game that is coordinated and documented on the Internet. You take Orwell's novel *1984* from the literature section of a public library and put it in the politics or economics section.

Jane McGonigals analog game *Ministry of Reshelving*.
@ Jane McGonigal, 2005

Here, games become what they should be today – instruments for opening up new spaces for the imagination, not between man and machine but between man and man, motivating them towards a different, freer life. And despite the high surveillance and potential for standardisation, fast multiple digital communication reveals opportunities for lighting tactical interventions by a highly networked gaming community endowed with little official power but high technical and cultural knowledge.

1 HTTP://EN.WIKIPEDIA.ORG/WIKI/WILLIAM_CROWTHER, HTTP://EN.WIKIPEDIA.ORG/WIKI/WILLIAM_CROWTHER
2 HTTP://EN.WIKIPEDIA.ORG/WIKI/KENTUCKY" HTTP://EN.WIKIPEDIA.ORG/WIKI/KENTUCKY
3 HTTP://SLURL.COM/SECONDLIFE/CULTUREREGION/132/118/75/
4 Cf. JAMES KORRIS, "ENDER'S GAME", IN: VON BORRIES, WALZ AND BÖTTGER, SPACE TIME PLAY, BASEL/BERLIN/BOSTON 2007.

Architecture is an obstacle. The topography of a city is structured in different levels of skills – from "beginner" to "expert".
© Apply Pictures

...similar to the game *Skate*.
© Electronic Arts

Le Saut dans le vide, The Leap into the Void, 5, rue Gentil-
Bernard, Fontenay-aux-Roses, October 1960. Artistic action by
Yves Klein, (photo montage). Title of the work by Yves Klein that
appeared in his newspaper *Dimanche – Le journal d´un seul jour*,
published Sunday 27 November 1960:
*"A man in space! The painter of space
throws himself into the void!"*

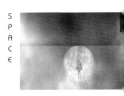

Parkour runner 2007.
© Benjamin Ellis

"*Understand that this art has been created by a few soldiers in Vietnam to escape or reach: and this is the spirit I'd like parkour to keep. You have to make the difference between what is useful and what is not in emergency situations. Then you'll know what is parkour and what is not. So if you do acrobatics things on the street with no other goal than showing off, please don't say it's parkour. Acrobatics existed a long time before parkour.*"

— *DAVID BELLE*
("Founder" of Parkour)

FUNCTION
FOLLOWS
FORM

– DREW HARRY, DIETMAR OFFENHUBER, JUDITH DONATH
SOCIABLE MEDIA GROUP, MIT MEDIA LAB

"Well, I have finally bought land and a farmhouse on Tuscany Island. The situation is gorgeous - I'm on a slope down from the Tuscan castle that stands at the centre of the land, so I have the castle behind me, and gentle hills in front of me, running down to the sea, where I have access to the landing stage. The water front itself is public, but if I want, I can keep a small boat pulled up on the shore and ready for when I want to go sailing (although I might just rezz it when I want it)." [1]

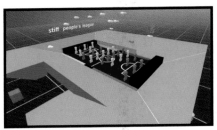

Analog vs. digital!
The Stiff People´s League
soccer table interface for
controlling the virtual
figures. The stadium in
Second Life is projected
onto the table.
When avatars run into the
ball, they automatically
kick it.
© ALL IMAGES BY THE AUTHORS

THE FUNCTIONAL AND THE SYMBOLIC

On a social level, buildings have the purpose of constraining behavior. In a very physical way, they direct our movement into certain trajectories or prevent us from going to certain places. They keep certain spaces dry and warm, while leaving others cold and wet. They keep certain people out, or other people in. Further, buildings also have the potential to induce behavior and influence our attitude. In a church, people start to whisper, but in a bar they'll need to shout to be heard. Taken to an extreme, Bentham's Panopticon enforced the discipline of its inmates by means of the centrally located but invisible wardens.[2] This control is accomplished by means of an architectural rhetoric with social implications. For example, the acoustics in a cathedral cause noises to echo, disturbing everyone else in the church and inviting disapproval from other patrons. As a result, visitors quickly learn that appropriate behavior in that space is to whisper.

In the virtual realm, the existence of a "building" is purely symbolic. It is a reference to a real-world structure, created in a space where none of the utilitarian functions – protection from the elements, air circulation, seating, etc. – have any relevance. Its symbolic functions bring legibility to what could otherwise be an incomprehensible abstract space.

We can understand this legibility as functioning much like the architectural logic of movie sets. Function follows form; the function of a place is unclear unless the building tells you what it is. A door on stage is not so much a functional connection between two spaces but a narrative device. This also works for more complex structures like cities. The organizational logic of E. Kettelhut's[3] design for the film *Metropolis* is immediately understood as a picture of class differences. This principle, the inscription of a narrative into a spatial structure, is what Norman M. Klein calls a "scripted space",[4] architectural space that is experienced according to a spatial movie script.
This legibility works in two primary ways: buildings in Second Life tell us both about how their creator expects them to be used, and also how their owner wants to be perceived by others.

The rhetoric of space places individual behavior into context and renders it either appropriate or inappropriate in much the same way as we see it in the real world. Not only is architectural vocabulary highly exaggerated in order to make the message clear, there is also a strong expectation concerning the behavior of avatars.

The projects, viewed from below.

The function of a place is unclear unless the building tells you what it is. A generic mall in Second Life. Its architectural features draw predominantly from the patterns of physical malls.

What convinces people engaging in online worlds to replicate and follow these conventions in an environment where supposedly everything is possible? This effect is an interesting feature of literal virtual worlds like Second Life and would not be possible in a purely abstract virtual environment. One hardly would know by intuition what behavior is appropriate in a purely abstract virtual word.

VIRTUAL SOCIAL ARCHITECTURE

Based on our observations of Second Life, we have developed a series of projects that investigate the social role of architecture in a practical way. We present two of them here to serve as concrete examples of that role. The first project, Agree/Disagree Spaces, focuses on ways in which the creative abandonment of the physical limitations of real world meeting places might lubricate the process of achieving decision consensus. The Stiff People's League provides a mechanism for economic and social interaction between avatars and the real players of a table soccer game. In both these projects, we propose specific ways in which virtual architecture plays a big role in creating new kinds of social spaces that couldn't exist outside of a virtual environment like Second Life.

AGREE/DISAGREE SPACES

Through chairs, buildings, and avatars, the form elements in Second Life are quite strong. This is carried over into the design of meeting spaces. They usually have strongly corporate overtones with high backed chairs, wood tables, and projects. And yet, a meeting held standing up in a house or bar would have the same functionality. What's missing is a functional approach to the design of social architecture. In our work, we try to build social spaces that have the functional richness of offline spaces, but in ways that can be more naturally expressed in a virtual environment than in a physical space or on the web. One of our projects that neatly captures this approach is a series of designs for meeting rooms. One benefit of working in a virtual environment is that spaces can be fluid and dynamic; because it's easy to change the design of the space and its functional attributes, we are free to design spaces for very specific kinds of interactions and then switch between them as our goals change. This is in contrast to physical spaces where the space itself is designed to be generic, and we use furniture and technology to try to adapt the room (with varying levels of success) to different purposes. We have started with a simple agree/disagree space for discussing a single-axis concept like whether to approve funding for a project, hire a new employee, or adopt a new technology.

The agree/disagree space encourages people involved in the meeting to use their physical position in the space as a social signal. The space is divided into four major zones. The agree/disagree area is very much like a traditional sports field with zones labeled "agree" and "disagree." It provides a space for people to position their avatars on a continuum within the zones to show their attitudes about the issue under discussion. The fluid self-arrangement of people based on their opinions provides a literal basis for seeing "where someone is coming from", and the status of the group's attempt to reach consensus. The virtual space of the field is therefore connected in a real-time fashion to the intellectual space of the discussion. Furthermore, you know that the people near you on the continuum agree with you more than people elsewhere on the field. Of course, not everyone always wants to reveal their opinion about the issue at hand. Literally "on the sidelines" of the main agree/disagree field is an area for people to position themselves to participate in the discussion without taking a stand. Still further from the field is an observation area for people who just want to watch but not play a role in the meeting. Finally, there is a platform for the moderator with controls to manage properties about the space itself.

The virtuality of the space allows us also to include a set of social utilities to support the continuous presentation of the contributions and shifting viewpoints of each participant. For this application, we have focused most on portraying the history of movements and conversation in the space, which serve to augment each avatar's presence in the space. The first step is to show how long each avatar has been standing in their current position. When an avatar pauses for a while, a transparent column will slowly rise out of the ground. The longer they stay there, the taller and thinner the column gets. When they move, the column will slowly shrink and eventually disappear. In this way, avatars leave a temporary mark on the space with their presence, and other people can use this signal to better understand what their position means. Their tall column would suggest they are steadfast in their support for something, or that they're not really paying attention. These different meanings can be disambiguated using other contextual information like what they're saying or whether they're idle. When an avatar in this space moves around, a path in space is drawn behind them. This makes movement a more explicit signal. Even if another person wasn't watching when they moved, a record of their movement stays in the space for a while before fading away. The space also records "spoken" contributions in text boxes that appear and then stack above the head of the avatar. This creates a visualization of chat over the course of the meeting, displaying what was said, when it was said, and where in the room the avatar was when they said it. Finally, the floor of the agree/disagree field displays the current average vote, as well as its deviation. Like chat messages, a representation of the group's collective view also floats up into the sky, providing more context about the overall feeling of the avatars in the space over time.

These social utilities create a space in which people's interactions with the space represent a new kind of social vocabulary based on position. This is just one way in which you can combine social utilities with the design of the space to create a specific kind of social space. There are other important ways in which the room might affect the behavior of people in it. Archiving can be turned on or off by the moderator for quick, off-the-record sessions. Avatars can be made anonymous, disconnecting chat from people's identity to change the social dynamics of the conversation. Various data about participation can also be visualized in the space or on the avatars to encourage different participation patterns. The space is rich with opportunities for adjusting the social functionality of the space to influence the behavior of people inside it along with the process and ultimate success of reaching decisions.

Are you on my side?
The fluid self-arrangement of people based on their opinions provides a literal basis for seeing "where someone is coming from" and the status of the group's attempt to reach consensus. People using the agree/disagree space, where people that are in the space send signals about their attitudes regarding the discussion topic. Traces in the sky visualize people's movements in the space.

STIFF PEOPLE'S LEAGUE

Virtual environments have never been completely separate from their offline counterparts. Indeed, the boundary between the virtual and physical world is often quite porous, relatively freely allowing the movement of money, identity, and social networks.[5] Still, people are interacting on the same terms and through the same interface. If socially significant activity is taking place in virtual environments (and we believe it is), then it is unreasonable to expect that there will be only one way for people to interact with other people in a virtual world. The Stiff People's League is a cooperative game between the virtual and physical world with some ironic undertones. In order to play, a team of avatars is recruited from within Second

Life to play for one of the two teams. When these avatars run into the ball, they automatically kick it. They can control the direction of the kick by approaching the ball from different directions. The players at the soccer table can only control the lateral movement of the rods, using the table's existing rods as the interface. This gives them the power to interfere with the movement of the ball and the avatars: they can block the ball, block the movement of avatars, hit the ball sideways, and push avatars sideways. The physical players can't spin the rods, so they have to rely on their team of avatars to support them by pushing the ball forward.

In this mixed reality construct, the rules and conditions of the game are a matter of negotiation between the two worlds. The real players need the virtual players to play the game, and each kind of player interacts with the game in very different ways. The physical players face disconcerting restrictions. In order to be successful, they must rely on the cooperation and skill of the avatars because their control in the game world is limited to a few clearly defined channels. Importantly, the soccer ball exists only in the virtual world, so the game is very much native to Second Life, and the physical players can only interact indirectly. This privileges the virtual players over the real players.

The project plays on a very common notion of animism, where the tokens in a game are alive and equipped with their own personality. Take for example the cricket game in *Alice in Wonderland*: the cricket bats used in this game are flamingos, while the ball is a hedgehog, living creatures that have to pretend they are objects. However, when they get bored with this role they start to misbehave and complicate the running game. This possibility for misbehavior and cheating is one of the more poetic advantages of Second Life as a place for games, when compared to typical computer games where rules are immutably executed by the machine. While the virtual players are reduced to the role of impersonating game figures, the balance of power and control between the virtual and physical worlds is not prescribed from the beginning.

To compensate the virtual players for playing for the real players, they are paid by the real players. Real players can offer more money to attract better players. By converting euros into Linden dollars, being a soccer player will be one of the most lucrative non-technical jobs in Second Life. This is an ironic commentary on the emerging labor model of virtual offshoring, that is, simple low-paid jobs performed by anonymous workers from within games and virtual worlds without any kind of responsibility to the employer.

One can imagine this concept of virtual work extended from the world of online environments to basically all domains of our lives. We are surrounded by pictorial or animated representations of persons. What if the avatar appearing in the channel selection menu of your digital TV is not a programmed character with artificial intelligence but actually controlled by a worker from a developing country, helping you configure your television? There is no reason why these jobs should serve only other residents; avatar workers could mediate a new wave of immigration, this time from the virtual world to the real world, playing interactive characters that increasingly appear in our lives.

But beyond this dystopian vision, the virtual participants of Stiff People's League have considerable power to influence the conditions of the whole game. Unlike a game world in which code is law, Second Life is better understood as a place where games happen. This gives it a very analog feel, and creates an environment where there is the possibility of ad hoc negotiation of rules, and cheating. In the Stiff People's League, this accentuates the virtual player's agency. The soccer game is being played in their world and with that world's rules. Much like a real soccer pitch, the space itself enforces few rules and the game exists in the collective understanding of its players.

SOCIAL UTILITIES

In these projects, we have created a set of technical systems that support different kinds of social interactions in the space. We think of these as social utilities, effectively the transportation, communication, and plumbing of a virtual environment. We believe that by augmenting virtual spaces with these sorts of services, virtual architecture can better support different types of interactions.

It is important to provide effective social utilities for creating and maintaining a sense of history in virtual spaces. The first step is to recreate some of the ways in which physical space aggregates history; stair steps show wear, dust accumulates in places that aren't swept, and graffiti artists co-opt spaces for personal expression. This sense of history is a powerful tool for us to interpret spaces. These issues have been explored in other interfaces. For example, the Edit wear / read wear project[6] made visible the use patterns of individuals accessing text files in collaborative work situations.

In a virtual environment, though, we can go much further than just emulating the aggregative properties of physical space. Certainly, it would be useful to create virtual spaces that wear away over time or collect dust. But we can also make spaces that collect the words of people in them in a variety of ways. We can make spaces that grow when people visit them and shrink when they're gone. For a collaborative design process, a space can maintain copies of itself that behave like a physical wiki.[7] In a presentation space, the presenter's slides could literally unfold into a discussion space for conversations after the lecture. These are just a few of many ways that aggregating history into physical spaces can be a powerful tool. Indeed, leveraging the history of spaces in novel ways forms the foundation for many of the social utilities we propose in this framework.

The presence of other people in Second Life is central to what sets it apart from other media, and so perhaps the most obvious way to make new kinds of social spaces is to make them respond to the presence of people within them. This can be useful both for people currently occupying the space (the room might grow to accommodate more people) as well as for people outside the space (showing at a glance what parts of a space are occupied).

The history of presence can also be quite useful. Spaces in Second Life are often abandoned and usually leave few traces of previous activities. Spaces that had huge crowds in them could be littered with bits from the conversation, or people could leave imprints where they were standing or sitting. Maybe there are even representations of the most talkative people in the space. We can also make spaces that are aware of their futures through the use of billboards and other messaging techniques. However it is accomplished, having spaces that are aware of the people inside them increases the legibility of the space for people who experience them alone and helps the navigability of space by giving cues about where people are now, have been, or will be.

1 "A Farmhouse in Tuscany", Prim Perfect. http://primperfectblog.wordpress.com/2007/08/19/a-farmhouse-in-tuscany/ (accessed September 18, 2007).

2 Michel Foucault, Discipline and Punish: The Birth of the Prison. New York 1979.

3 D. Neumann, and D. Albrecht, Film Architecture: Set Designs from Metropolis to Blade Runner. Munich 1996.

4 Norman Klein, The Vatican to Vegas: The History of Special Effects. New York and London 2004.

5 E. Castronova, Synthetic Worlds: The Business and Culture of Online Games. Chicago 2006.

6 W.C. Hill, et al., "Edit wear and read wear", Proceedings of the SIGCHI conference on Human factors in computing systems, 1992, p. 3–9.

7 T.S. Shaw, Studio Wikitecture, Second Life @ the Design Museum in London / RIBA Architecture Week 2007, http://archsl.wordpress.com/2007/06/14/second-life-the-design-museum-for-riba-architecture-week-june-2007/.

THE GESTURE OF SITTING IN VIRTUAL SPACE

Panel discussion at the
Metaverse07 conference.
© Bokowsky & Laymann

EXPLORING the virtual landscapes of Second Life, a new visitor might be surprised by the large number of chairs in the environment and the prominence of the "sit" button in the context menu. Do avatars get tired from all the flying and need to rest frequently? In real spaces, chairs support our bodies, fulfilling an important physical function. Chairs let us comfortably spend time in the same place for long periods of time. Because the role of chairs in the real world derives solely from the physiological needs of real humans, it seems ironic that a virtual environment should have chairs in it at all; avatars don't get tired, so why would they need chairs? The answer lies in the social function of showing your commitment to not moving which makes chairs, virtual or real, excellent examples of rich social objects from which we can learn a number of lessons about designing virtual social spaces.

Throughout cultural history, chairs stand for, more than any other furniture, social order – or disorder. The arrangement and design of seating immediately implies the existence or absence of hierarchies and modes of interaction. This can be easily illustrated by looking at the differences between the seating in an auditorium, a dining room, or a courtroom. By articulating the ways that chairs in Second Life function, we can explain the potential complexity of communication in a virtual environment.

Sitting in a chair, real or virtual, communicates a commitment to the space; a seated person is settled in, not likely to leave, and engaged with what's going on in this space. In contrast, people or avatars that are standing feel transient. They're just observing until they sit down. In Second Life, sitting down sends a similar message as taking off a coat or setting down a purse. Also, how the chairs are arranged in a space and where someone chooses to sit is important. A circle of chairs implies a discussion group, while an amphitheatre layout implies a presentation or performance. People can also choose to sit relative to other people to communicate their involvement level; an avatar might sit near the back in a presentation space to show they're not connected with the groups of people at the front of the space.

This richness makes chairs one of the most socially successful objects in Second Life. Although some aspects of the function of physical chairs don't make sense in a virtual environment, the bulk of the meaning encoded in chairs and interactions surrounding chairs can be expressed successfully in a virtual environment. Chairs are a model for the level of social significance we think should be expected from Second Life objects.

Chairs are a real-world metaphor that works well in a virtual environment, but they are by no means perfect. Translating an object into a virtual environment involves some sort of conceptual abstraction, and the choices you make in that abstraction can limit its effectiveness. Virtual chairs, for instance, hold their position and can't be adjusted to show your closeness with other people in the room. You can't use them to hold a coat. You can't etch graffiti into them. This is not to say that these functions are core to being a chair. Nonetheless, there are ways to provide ways for avatars to "sit" while still allowing them to serve other functions.

MOEL Sessel und Sofa. Design: Inga Sempé. Katalog: www.ligne-roset.de

ligne roset

Leben Sie schön.

FACTS & FIGURES

Out of 126 entries four winners were chosen by the jury at the Ars Electronica 2007: Meylenstein, Adam Nash, Max Mooswitzer, DC Spensley

———

Out of the four projects **Meylensteins "Living Cloud"** won the PUBLIC VOTING via the internet. The prize ceremony took place at the UNESCO World Cultural Heritage Zollverein Essen.

———

MEMBERS OF THE JURY
Pascal Schöning, Shumon Basar, Melinda Rackham, Mathieu Wellner, Tor Lindstrand, Stephan Doesinger

———

CRITERIA
Definitions and questions for the jury at the Ars Electronica Linz 2007.

STYLE
Is the project cool? Is it sexy? Just a subjective evaluation!

INNOVATION
Seen that – done that?! Visual utopia - is it something new?

SCRIPTING
How clever are the functions used? How complex is the programming – and how easy is it to use? Are the scriptings inspiring?

SPATIAL CONCEPT & STORY
What is the concept about? Is it a cool spatial idea? Is the story convincing? Does the project support interaction with other people and avatars?

INTEGRATED MEDIA
Use of images, videos, music within the SL environment. Is it a "3D-MySpace"?

CROSS MEDIA POTENTIAL
Are there any links to external media in "first life"? e. g. connections to mobile phones, GPS systems, etc. ? (at least conceptually)

IMAGINATIVE POWER
Is the project inspiring? What is the "mood" of the project? Are there any cultural references to art forms such as films, art, etc. Is there a cool ingenious narrative?

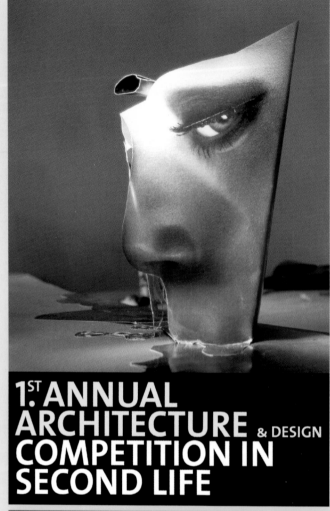

1ST ANNUAL ARCHITECTURE & DESIGN COMPETITION IN SECOND LIFE

Virtually analog: Competition poster based on cut & fold paper models from magazines such as *Vogue, Penthouse, Elle*, etc. by Stephan Doesinger. (Original size ca. 5cm). The models are the structural and aesthetic basis for real 1:1 buildings.
© Stephan Doesinger & Ydo Sol

1ST ANNUAL ARCHITECTURE & DESIGN COMPETITION IN SECOND LIFE

1ST ANNUAL ARCHITECTURE & DESIGN COMPETITION IN SECOND LIFE

RESULTS FROM THE FIRST ARCHITECTURE & DESIGN COMPETITION IN SECOND LIFE

THE WORLD'S BEST ARCHITECTURE IN SECOND LIFE

– MEYLENSTEIN, MAX MOOSWITZER, ADAM NASH, DC SPENSLEY AND

CARSTEN LUBITZ, SCOPE CLEAVER, ROGER JEGERLEHNER, THOMAS RASOKAT & MARKUS BOKOWSKY, JON BROUCHOUD, DAVID DENTON, ALES BURSIC, OVOS REALTIME 3D, DINAH LIM FAT & LIE XIN WONG, JOCHEN HOOG, STEFANO OSTINELLI, PIXELBREEZE LTD, LESTER CLARK, PETER SCHARMÜLLER, ARCO ROSCA, KATE ALLEN, STEPHAN BOLCH, NOÉMI ÖRDÖG, NADIA CLEMENT, MECHTHILD SCHMIDT-FEIST, OLAF FINKBEINER, IBRAHIM ABDELHADY, BRAD KLIGERMAN & JAMIL MEHDAOUI, UNINETTUNO, TED MIKULSKI, PDINSL, ALFREDO SABATO, PAULO FRIAS, MARC FROHN & SASCHA GLASL, VERA BIGHETTI, GISELLE BEIGUELMAN, JULIANA CONSTATINO & ELAINE SANTOS, CEZARY OSTROWSKI, LUTZ WAGNER, STEFAN WEISS.

BETWEEN... *by Stephan Doesinger*

BETWEEN DISCOVERY AND FREE FALL?

Many contemporary architects have long harboured a wish to suspend the laws of gravity. Coop Himmelblau's stab at the task took the shape of a whale catapulting its body out of the water. The idea was to freeze-frame the moment before this monumentally heavy body fell back into the sea. The sensation thereby captured would then inform the design of the building. The building would float over people's heads like a three-dimensional photo and stick its tongue out at gravity. After all, gravity is full of risks. So, were the whale not to drop back to where it came from along a Heisenberg curve of movement, it would not have to hang suspended in the air as a trophy of interrupted movement.

Now, in cartoon films, one of the characters, e.g. Daffy Duck, might happen to career over a cliff edge, and only falls at the moment when he notices the yawning abyss below. There are many different versions of this motif in the genre. Sometimes Daffy tries to quietly make it back to the safety of the clifftop, sometimes he tries to fly with withered arms. But generally, the moment of realisation is the moment of the inevitable free fall. In Second Life, this fall never occurs, nor even the movement preceding it. The salto mortale moment is not there, so that the calculated point of impact is also absent. There is no fall line. The buildings float around motionlessly – apparently anchored by invisible stays. Only a few creative scriptings set the floating structures into controlled motion, changing shapes and colours like a cuttlefish.

BETWEEN PHYSICAL AND VIRTUAL

If nonetheless you get into the embarrassing position of falling over the edge with the avatar, there is always a soft landing. Though this term sounds very light-footed, it does not conceal the weight of fear that it actually expresses. The term features constantly in US business news these days, in reference to the fear of the next banking disaster. Even if only virtual numbers tumble, these still have massive effects on our physical reality. In a life where digital gravity is more dangerous than the earth, it is no wonder that this generates a new sense of existence. Possibly we are sitting in a house of real brick and mortar whose value or credit is about as real as a building in Second Life.

BETWEEN TWO GENERATIONS

For the generation of architects who grew up with computer games, the whale would have changed into a cloud or a space ship as it leapt. In any case, the expected splash effect in slow motion,

when the whale drops back into the water, would be more interesting than the freeze-frame.

Between the generation of architects, artists and creative people who grew up with computer games there is a yawning invisible cultural gap separating them from the previous generation that becomes more and more evident with increasing distance.

That is not only because computer games and virtual worlds (offline or online) are steadily becoming a key global medium economically. Numerous young architects earn their money on graduating not (only) by building real buildings but as games designers, doing visualisations or working on animation films. For them, computers are culturally hybrid machines, the central tool of both spatial experience and communications/design as well.

BETWEEN PRIVATE AND PUBLIC

Perhaps it is also because of the cultural gap that only professional architects and designers took part in this competition, although it was open to everyone. At the beginning of the experiment, this was not at all clear. The point of the competition was to stick a seismographic probe into the electronic ground of Second Life so as to discover what buildings the younger generation of architects dreamt about. What would their architectural utopias in Second Life have to tell us?

In the course of the competition, it turned out that the various categories such as private homes, commercial, high-rise and special projects were irrelevant because there was no point to them in virtual architecture. In fact, for many of those who took part in this competition, architecture is a three-dimensional interface and the city is a sports ground. In their minds, all physical buildings are as soft as in the film Matrix. With the computer, any space can be entered from the outside. In order to pass through walls, you don't even need to be a supernatural figure like the angel in Wings of Desire. A password is all you need ...

Categories such as private and public have also lost terra firma beneath them. Many buildings in Second Life were thus virtually hidden away in airy heights, or like the winning project only existed as a cloud.

Buildings as an "extension of the body" have acquired a new virtual dimension ...

LIVING CLOUD

To find me in SL Search for \"Creatina Ferraris\"

Name:

Meylenstein   *Winning Project*

Real Life Profession:

Architect / Designer

RL Country / City: Effort / hrs.

Berlin / Germany   3840

About:

"My name is Creatina Ferraris and my LIVING CLOUD is always with me. It is my private home. I take it with me. I don't need to buy land. I don't need to pay rent. I really live in it."

"You should see me with my LIVING CLOUD in action, You should see interactions with SL residents, ... it's a lot of fun..."

In order to redefine "home" and "privacy" in SL-context, I would say, my LIVING CLOUD performs any task my living requirements are asking for. It is to set up new ideas or concepts of "being" which can be exposed in architecture as well. Architecture is more than building houses, also in real life...
My main issue as an RL- and SL-architect is to create new concepts according to the new "laws" defining SL rather than copying RL architecture into SL.
The new "laws" are for example the new locomotion possibilities, new gravity laws, new biological laws, etc. These new "laws" mean not only a diversification of living requirements but also a diversification of the relation between public spaces versus private space. Urban design needs to be questioned, but not necessarily.

The big opportunity that I can see in SL is not utilized yet.

Electronic Music ((◄

"There is no location for my living cloud.
My home is where I am!"

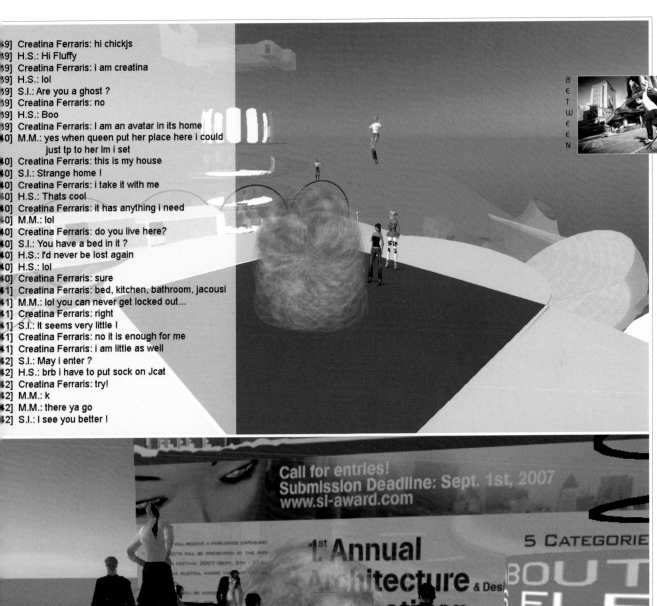

9] Creatina Ferraris: hi chickjs
9] H.S.: Hi Fluffy
9] Creatina Ferraris: i am creatina
9] H.S.: lol
9] S.I.: Are you a ghost ?
9] Creatina Ferraris: no
9] H.S.: Boo
9] Creatina Ferraris: I am an avatar in its home
0] M.M.: yes when queen put her place here i could
      just tp to her lm i set
0] Creatina Ferraris: this is my house
0] S.I.: Strange home !
0] Creatina Ferraris: i take it with me
0] H.S.: Thats cool
0] Creatina Ferraris: it has anything i need
0] M.M.: lol
0] Creatina Ferraris: do you live here?
0] S.I.: You have a bed in it ?
0] H.S.: I'd never be lost again
0] H.S.: lol
0] Creatina Ferraris: sure
1] Creatina Ferraris: bed, kitchen, bathroom, jacousi
1] M.M.: lol you can never get locked out...
1] Creatina Ferraris: right
1] S.I.: It seems very little !
1] Creatina Ferraris: no it is enough for me
1] Creatina Ferraris: i am little as well
2] S.I.: May i enter ?
2] H.S.: brb i have to put sock on Jcat
2] Creatina Ferraris: try!
2] M.M.: k
2] M.M.: there ya go
2] S.I.: I see you better !

B
E
T
W
E
E
N

Call for entries!
Submission Deadline: Sept. 1st, 2007
www.sl-award.com

1st Annual
Architecture & Desi

5 CATEGORIE

BOUT
ELE

LANDSCAPE DESIGN

FREESTYLE AND
SPECIAL PROJECTS

WHITENOISE

SURL: http://slurl.com/secondlife/klein/152/218/45/?title=WhiteNoise

Name:

Max Mooswitzer **Winning Project**

Real Life Profession:

Artist / Lecturer

RL Country / City: Austria / Vienna   **Effort / hrs.:** 25

About:

An experiment for non-human architecture in Second Life. This construct uses Freebie objects which are all set in white. The interesting views are when these objects join with others. With a tool we use, this building has just around 25 prims; normally it would have 1,000 prims. It is an ongoing project and will go into more "high-res" detail, we call it "Whitenoise". White Noise, a reference to random pattern and "Bildrauschen", which we as builders see working for hours and you think you get snowblind.

THINK DIFFERENT! Architecture in SL should not be the same as in the real world. Avatars don't need a roof; it never rains in Second Life...

FIRST ECONOMIES *by Shumon Basar, jury member*

WHEN I FIRST HEARD ABOUT the First Architecture Competition in Second Life, I thought: "Great!" Surely it would be interesting to design without gravity, without the obvious obligation to be sensible. Months later we jurors met in "First Life" and publicly trawled through the 126 entries. Generally speaking, the results were a little disappointing: tasteful minimalist villas, post-modern baroque functionalism, New Age organic mush. There was a strange and hard to explain ordinariness to the majority of entries.

However, one submission stood out. In this scenario, Second Life users were encouraged to dump "freebie" objects on a promontory, where they pile up. The designer of this process turns all the objects – teddy bears, plant pots, platonic shapes – white, and the result is a growing Pop agglomeration. The beauty of the project isn't what it looks like but that the material is based on freebies: detritus objects that have no monetary value. Amidst Second Life's re-enactment of global capitalism, where you don't get nuffin' for nuffin', this virtual construction process turns a loophole into a sculpture that is also a critique.

At this point, I ought to confess to a penchant I have recently developed. It's for the *Financial Times* at the weekend. I'd like to say it's because I assiduously follow the global markets. But the truth is I want to get my hands on the occasional large-format colour supplement which has one of the most beautifully functional titles ever: *How to Spend It*.

A typical opening double-page spread will be adorned by an advert for a yacht that is crashing heroically against the bracing Caribbean waves, whilst the skipper (presumably you, if you buy the yacht) grins with the self-satisfaction of someone that has it all, plus more. And *How to Spend It* is aimed precisely at yacht sailing, Breitling watch wearing, Brioni suit clad capitalists, the likes of which induce the most profound form of derision and jealousy by the rest of us.

Alas, I don't actually belong to this moneyed, fast-track set. No, I buy *How to Spend It* because there's a perverse enjoyment in the self-punishment of flicking through the absurd, reflective, inflated world of ultra luxury goods.

I detour through this luxury aside because perhaps I shouldn't have been surprised that the virtual "other" world of Second Life is already an immersive regime of capitalist forces, desires and limits. As I wandered through – a cross between Baudelaire and Lara Croft, without a penny in my pocket – I found I could engage with very little of what was on offer. It all cost Linden dollars. So, any dreams of dreaming up that yacht from the advert for free vanish completely.

The competition project that we all unanimously chose as a deserving winner provoked the necessity of Second Life to naturally emulate the First Economy that regulates everything in this flesh-ridden, gravity bound, poverty stricken, incongruous world we all live in when the LCD screen is switched off. What might a different First Economy other than the one we now assume is the only one left look like?

How to Spend It has an endearing and therefore dangerous charm in its brazen superficiality. Happiness is not complicated. Just sail along the frictionless waves of ever-better and never-ending consumer items, and you find that happiness is easy, in this, and in Second Life. Until someone reminds you that you've run out of credit.

Based on a version of 'The Object', published by Blueprint magazine, in November 2007.

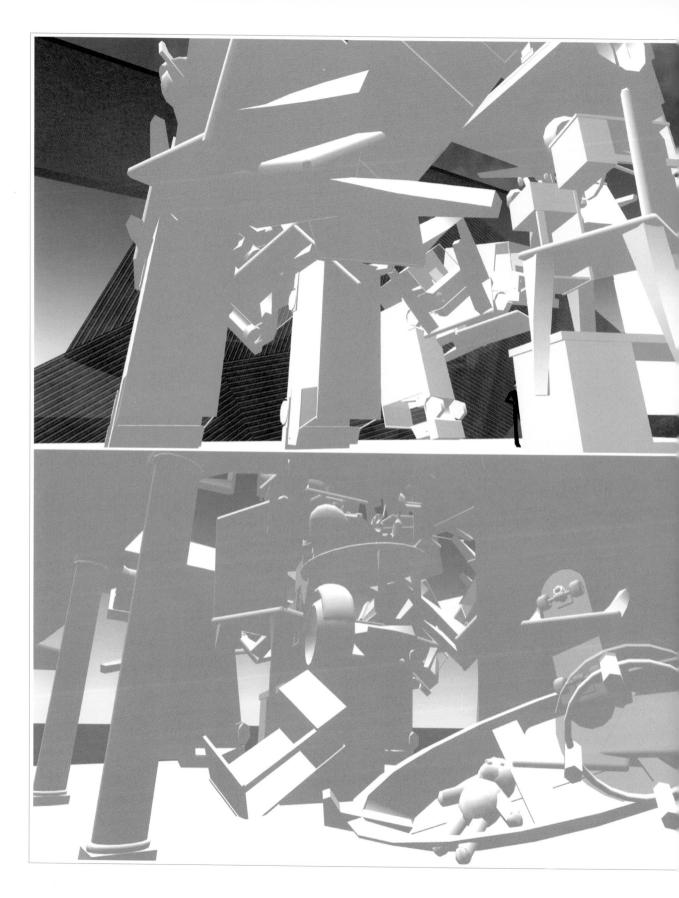

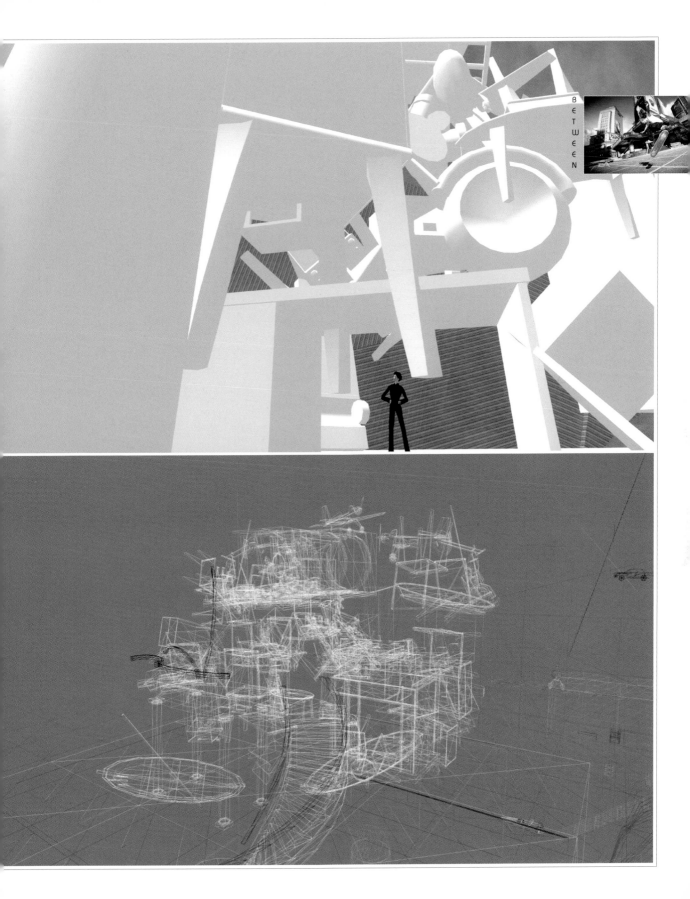

BETWEEN

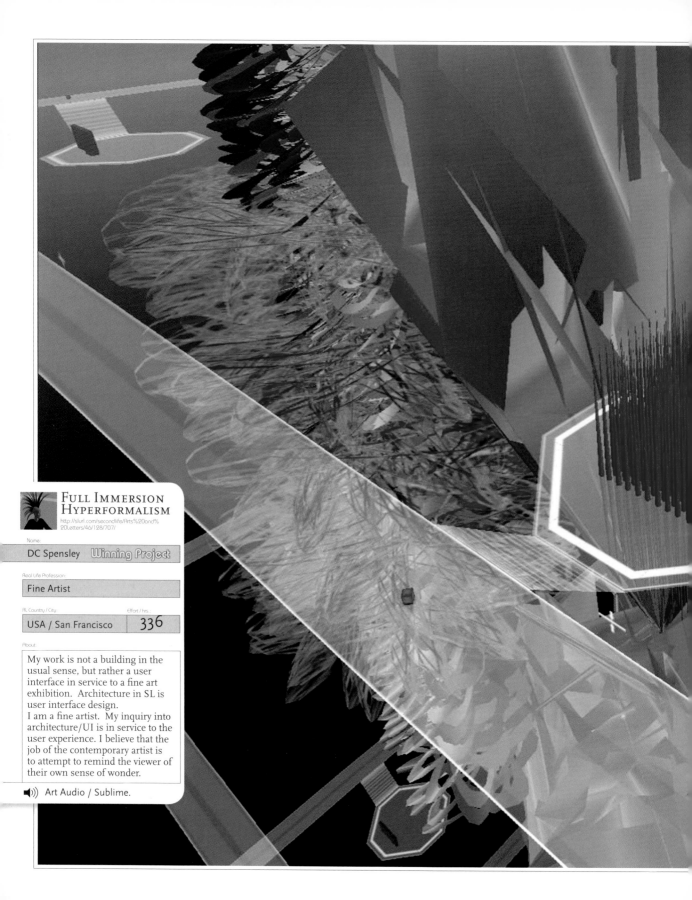

FULL IMMERSION HYPERFORMALISM

http://slurl.com/secondlife/Arts%20and%
20Letters/46/128/707/

Name:

DC Spensley *Winning Project*

Real Life Profession:

Fine Artist

RL Country / City:

USA / San Francisco

Effort / hrs.:

336

About:

My work is not a building in the usual sense, but rather a user interface in service to a fine art exhibition. Architecture in SL is user interface design.
I am a fine artist. My inquiry into architecture/UI is in service to the user experience. I believe that the job of the contemporary artist is to attempt to remind the viewer of their own sense of wonder.

🔊 Art Audio / Sublime.

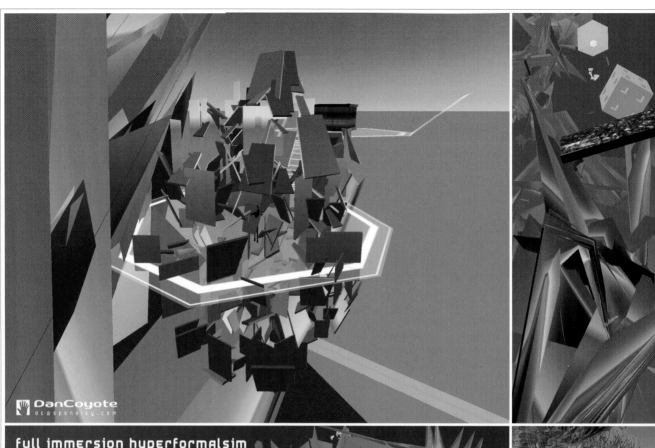

full immersion hyperformalsim

The foundational navigation artifice is called "stealth architecture" and refers to the use of semi-transparent "glass" walkways and pads to define areas of interest throughout the installation. This approach is flexible and modular and economical in that it employs few prim resources and reuses a small set of optimized textures.

Most importantly stealth architecture is invisible from below. Only the necessary faces of the pads are textured and visible. This reduces visual clutter and places emphasis on the content instead of the artifice.

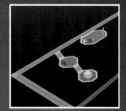

"Stealth Architecture"
(glass walkways, pads)

 DanCoyote

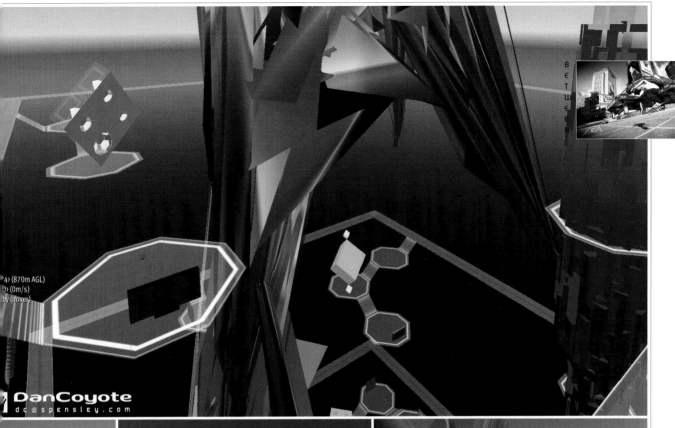

4› (870m AGL)
» (0m/s)
ty (flover)

DanCoyote
dc@spensley.com

BETWEEN

full immersion hyperformalsim

Clicking red cubes througout the exhibition
literally carries the viewer throgh the volume
of the space. There are 10 pre-programmed
nodes, but many more accssible by flying.
Free flight enhancement is availble in the
default teleport location.

Didactic signs (at right) display names and
theoretical rationale for sculptural objects.

Visit Selected
Exhibition Highlights
by CUBE!

Click cube, and select
a node. The cube will
sit you down and carry
you to that node.

DanCoyote
dc@spensley.com
plate 5 of 5

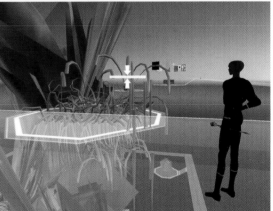

"...its Noodly Appendages" V
Close viewer interaction
turns spaghetti landscapes.

Seventeen Unsung Songs

SURL: http://slurl.com/secondlife/East%20of%
20Odyssey/37/89/32/

Name:

| Adam Nash | Winning Project |

Real Life Profession:

| Artist / Lecturer |

| RL Country / City: | Effort / hrs.: |
| Australia / Melbourne | 672 |

About:

The building Seventeen Unsung
Songs is a sim-wide, interactive,
immersive, audiovisual, spatial and
temporal artwork. The planing is a
long process of iterative audiovisual design, often in consultation
with Sugar Seville, the owner and
curator of the Odyssey island.
Perfection in design is achieved
when there is nothing left to take
away.
  I am an interactive experience
designer and designer of virtual
worlds, and teach this at university.
I recognise no distinction between
actual and virtual.

🔊)) Hardcore / Softcore / Jazz

"I recognise no distinction between
actual and virtual."

BETWEEN

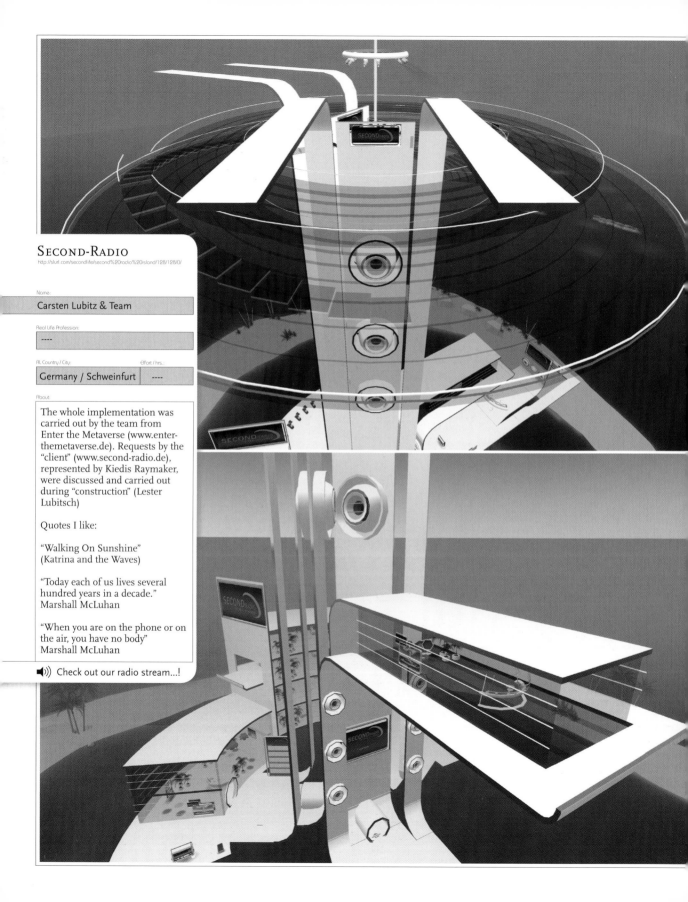

SECOND-RADIO

http://slurl.com/secondlife/second%20radio%20island/128/128/0/

Name:

Carsten Lubitz & Team

Real Life Profession:

RL Country / City: Effort / hrs.:

Germany / Schweinfurt   ----

About:

The whole implementation was carried out by the team from Enter the Metaverse (www.enter-themetaverse.de). Requests by the "client" (www.second-radio.de), represented by Kiedis Raymaker, were discussed and carried out during "construction" (Lester Lubitsch)

Quotes I like:

"Walking On Sunshine" (Katrina and the Waves)

"Today each of us lives several hundred years in a decade." Marshall McLuhan

"When you are on the phone or on the air, you have no body" Marshall McLuhan

🔊)) Check out our radio stream...!

SCDA
http://slurl.com/secondlife/SCDA/0/128/24/
?img=http%3A//

Name:

Scope Cleaver

Real Life Profession:

RL Country / City:

Second Life

Effort / hrs.:

240

About

Ultra modern stores for my furniture, divided in furniture for home, one for office and my own office in the middle.
For the planning, everything was done in SL, including the conceptual stage and sketches.

I like the mathematics in the geometry and the fluidity.

Ambient Music

STARFRUIT
SURL: http://slurl.com/secondlife/Starfruit/
33/131/23/

Name:
Roger Jegerlehner

Real Life Profession:
Senior R&D Engineer

RL Country / City:
CH / Bern

Effort / hrs.:
1464

About:

Starfruit is a venture at Swisscom Innovations with the vision of bridging virtual worlds like Second Life and real world.

In May 2007 Starfruit places a few virtual telephone booths in Second Life from which users in Second Life can send free SMS text messages to mobile phones anywhere in the world. A further possibility is teleporting (beaming) from one telephone booth to another. This allows users to discover and visit new and interesting places in Second Life. The telephone booths are free so interested users can take a virtual copy and place it on their land. In the first two months more than 300 virtual telephone booths have been placed all over Second Life.

A further service from Starfruit is the possibility to send real gifts from Second Life to real life. A Second Life user buys virtual flowers or chocolates in a Starfruit shop. These he can give to his girlfriend in Second Life. Then she can redeem the gift and will receive the flowers / chocolates delivered by our partner Fleurop to her real-life home. For the first time it is possible to send real gifts from Second Life...

This project has received a lot of media attention. Starfruit was on the Swiss television on 10vor10, In various Swiss newspapers and the in-world newspaper AvaStar. We have had positive feedback on our services, as stated in numerous blogs and from the Starfruit in-world community.

st★rfruit BETA
BRIDGING WORLDS

Gift service | TowerTalk | Free SMS | Discover

Gift Service

Would you like to surprise someone in Second Life and send them a real gift in real life... but you don't know their real postal address? Don't worry any more... we will take care of everything.

① Romeo buys virtual flowers in Second Life

② Romeo gives flowers to Juliet in Second Life

③ The real Juliet clicks on the virtual flowers and enters her postal address. Privacy guaranteed!

④ Gift is delivered to Juliet

⑤ Juliet gets REAL flowers in REAL life and is REALLY happy

Privacy
Romeo will never know the address of Juliet and vice-versa.

Other gifts
Premium chocolate 250g

Expand your virtual friendship into the real world!

WELTBILD

SURL: http://slurl.com/secondlife/
Weltbild/128/128/0

Name:
Thomas Rasokat / Markus Bokowsky

Real Life Profession:
Designer

RL Country / City:
Germany / Munich

Effort / hrs. :
2160

About:
The new Home of the RL company
Weltbild in Second Life.
Building steps:
- Mock up in SketchUp
- Details in Blender
- Textures with Photoshop

🔊)) FM4

"Become an active part of the community you are interested in!
Meet and collaborate with others!
Think freely!
Cross disciplines!"

CLICK HERE FOR A LANDMARK TO THE GALLERY OF REFLEXIVE ARCHITECTURE

BULB / REFLEXIVE ARCHITECTURE

http://slurl.com/secondlife/Architecture/191/110/601/
?title=Gallery%20of%20Reflexive%20Architecture

Name:
Jon Brouchoud

Real Life Profession:
Architect

RL Country / City: Effort / hrs.:
USA / Albany   5

About

This installation explores the idea that architecture in a virtual environment can transcend the rigid and static nature of physical architecture, and become more dynamic, reflexive and contextually responsive. As avatars move through this space, the architecture reacts to their presence by creating a bulb around each occupant that follows them as they move around. When avatars move together, the bulbs meld into a single integral space.

I collaborated with a scripter to help realize these ideas. After developing these scripts, I open-sourced them to the public.

The architecture is intended to encourage the avatars, fashion and design of occupants in expressing their own individual taste. This diversity of self-expression becomes a dynamic part of the composition.

Folk ((◉▶

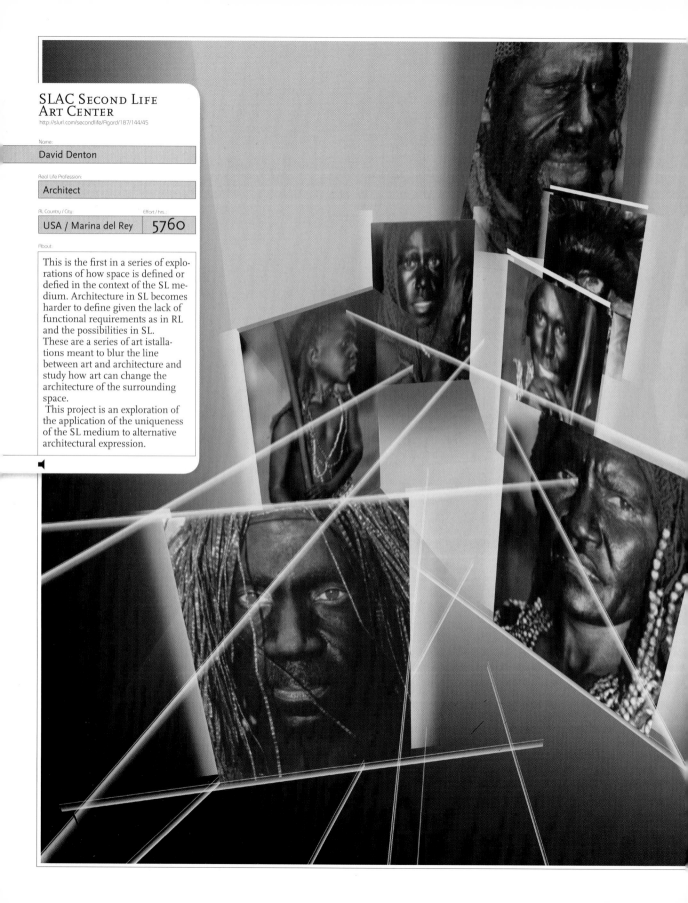

SLAC Second Life Art Center

http://slurl.com/secondlife/Agard/187/144/45

Name:
David Denton

Real Life Profession:
Architect

RL Country / City:
USA / Marina del Rey

Effort / hrs...
5760

About:
This is the first in a series of explorations of how space is defined or defied in the context of the SL medium. Architecture in SL becomes harder to define given the lack of functional requirements as in RL and the possibilities in SL.
These are a series of art istallations meant to blur the line between art and architecture and study how art can change the architecture of the surrounding space.
This project is an exploration of the application of the uniqueness of the SL medium to alternative architectural expression.

BETWEEN

ARENA

SURL: http://slurl.com/secondlife/Artists%20Island/77/52/21/?x=512&u=1024&img=http%5A//lh5.google.com/thinzdiff/RsmBTJu3bnl/AAAAAAAAAI0/n-cGmuD.klk/s144/LandofThinXSpear01.jpg&title=Land%20of%20ThinX

Name:

Ales Bursic

Real Life Profession:

Designer for industrial robotics

RL Country / City:	Effort / hrs.:
France / Paris	336

About:

Starting with... doing nothing, then thinking... Then with the help of ACAD and CATIA software to provide the main points and coordinates, and the first quick glance of how it will/should look like is pretty much my standard procedure.

I am presenting my vision of a multifunctional stadium/arena in SL (1:10 scale model). The arena is just big enough to hold a standard football field. As I see some constant problems with land I have decided to put this building in the air. Buildings in SL should carry all multimedia options available in SL. Rotating blades are just fancy gadgets enriching the appearance of the stadium.

🔊)) all kind of music except rap

"Dream your best and wildest dream and make it happen....in SL!"

FLOATING MONOLITH

SURL: http://slurl.com/secondlife/Baedal/236.389/80.1368

Name:

Ovos Realtime 3D

Real Life Profession:

Designer / Architect

RL Country / City: Effort / hrs.:

Austria / Vienna   480

About

The building is a floating monolith residing on a spiral covered
with numerous organic silver-
ish objects. After entering the
monolith you\'ll find yourself in
a dazzling world of mesmerizing
moire effects. Float through the
space and feel the walls around
you becoming alive.

FUSION DREAMS

http://slurl.com/secondlife/rmit/180/75

Name:

Dinah Lim Fat & Lie Xin Wong

Real Life Profession:

Interior Design students

RL Country / City: Effort / hrs.:

Australia / Melbourne   2160

About:

Fusion Dreams is a design project on the RMIT island. It is the abstract representation of a library of emotions. It perpetuates the idea of the state of dreaming as a performance of the mind, where the collection of emotions start to interweave and become a totally new experience. The emotion data and sound collection of the library then lies dormant within the entire sculpture, until an avatar activates the panels and cubes where the data codes are stored.

We like simplicity, the use of natural light, like Tadao Ando or Jean Nouvel, creativity and imagination like Gaudi.

◀)) Jazz

```
//This segment contains the individual states of each emotional data.
//Script has been clipped and only critical portions are shown.
//The immediate following is the typical full segment for an emotional script.

//full state script
state excite

//Cube dance type 1

integer counter;                          state_entry()
integer second;                           {    Handle = llListen(10, "", NULL_KEY, "");
vector startScale;                        // If another command is issued, event transits to the new state    }
integer Handle;                           listen(integer channel, string name, key id, string message)
                                              {    if (message == "off")
default                                            {    llListenControl(Handle, FALSE);    }
{                                               if (message == "excite")
    state_entry()                                    {    state excite;    }
    {                                           if (message == "sad")
        // start listening on channel 10 for control commands        {    state sad;    }
        Handle = llListen(10, "", NULL_KEY, "");    if (message == "lust")
        // get original scale of cubes                  {    state lust;    }
        startScale = llGetScale();              if (message == "fear")
    }                                                {    state fear;    }
    listen(integer channel, string name, key id, string message)    if (message == "empty")
    {                                                {    state empty;    }
        if (message == "off")                  }
            {    llListenControl(Handle, FALSE);    }    // Sets up an event every 1 second
        if (message == "excite")               timer()
            {    state excite;    }                 {    second++;
        if (message == "sad")                          // sets cubes to red color
            {    state sad;    }            vector prim_color = < 1.0, 0, 0 >;
        if (message == "lust")                         llSetColor( prim_color, ALL_SIDES );
            {    state lust;    }                      // Makes cubes dance with random scale but constant beat
        if (message == "fear")                         float new_scale = llFrand( 6.0 );
            {    state fear;    }                       llSetScale(< 0.5, 0.5, new_scale > );
        if (message == "empty")
            {    state empty;    }            // stops animation after 30 seconds and
    }                                         // scales cube back to original size
}                                             if ( second > 30 )
                                                      {    while ( llVecDist( llGetScale(), startScale ) > 0.001 )
                                                        {    llSetScale( startScale );    }
                                                        // return object to ready state.
                                                        llResetScript();
                                                      }
                                              }
```

```
//
// The script has been clipped.
// Only the timer event script which is critical is shown.

//typical state
state sad
{    timer()
    {    second++;
        // sets cubes to grey color
        vector prim_color = < 0.2, 0.2, 0.2 >;
        llSetColor( prim_color, ALL_SIDES );
// Makes cubes stunted and change scales to sinusoidal
// formula below
        float new_scale = llFrand(2.0) * llFabs(llSin( second/5 )) ;
        llSetScale(< 0.5, 0.5, new_scale > );
```

"Because Second Life is a game with a lot of advantages like scripts, sounds, interaction... the design process can be really complex but fascinating. Second Life is a new medium for designing."

FUSION DREAMS

Global Engine

Excite1
Excite2
Amaze1
Amaze2
Amaze3
Confuse1
Confuse2
Fear1
Fear2
Fear3
Sad1
Sad2
Lust
Anger
Empty

Teleport to next space

DJ Platform

Local Engine

Symphony Mode
The Virtual Jockey Space is the console to conduct the performance of the library of emotions. It acts as a global search engine where upon touching an emotion cube will activate an event in the sculpture space, causing the 'data' to manifest, as well as play a sound that responds to the emotion. Mix your own pieces of emotions to create different results.

Exploring Mode
Explore the sculpture space to discover a collection of spatial experiences nested within the overall performance. Interacting with different items within each respective space will create different effects and activate events, which then becomes a local search for the emotion data matter.

ARCHDIPLOMA

http://slurl.com/secondlife/orch%20tu.wien/7/0/37/?img=http%3A//
www.otelierpr

Name:

Jochen Hoog & team

Real Life Profession:

Architect / lecturer

RL Country / City: Effort / hrs.:

Austria / Vienna   1440

About:

The presented project is a virtual
exhibition space of the archdi-
ploma2007. This is an exhibition
of the best diploma works from
graduates at the TU Vienna of the
last two years. The different works
are rebuilt in SL by reducing the
geometry and simplifying textures
and colours. The visitor of the
virtual exhibition enters the island
at one corner and is surrounded
by the presented projects. All
projects are placed on the island
randomly (and randomly twisted);
they stay for a while, vanish and
are "reborn" again. This ongoing
process produces a deeply complex
environment. The objects melt
together, they overlap and pen-
etrate each other, unless the visitor
enters one of the buildings, then
the process is halted, the building
remains still and can be explored.
The result is a reactive environment. The archdiploma2007
becomes a hyper-exhibition. Real
"virtual", the projects become real
in a virtual environment. The exhibition becomes a hybrid media:
cinematographic in its appearance,
digital on the level of its material
and computational in its logic.

Team members:
Prof. Manfred Wolff-Plottegg
Johannes Sperlhofer

FOUR ELEMENTS
http://slurl.com/secondlife/Architecture/
115/172/453

Name:

Stefano Ostinelli

Real Life Profession:

Architect

RL Country / City: Effort / hrs :

Italy / Cernobbio   **168**

About

It is composed of four elements:
a room (earth), a balcony (sky),
a pool (water) and a tower (fire).
They are connected by a path that
is something like two stairwells.
The room has a bottom like a ship
(you can look at its inside through
the grate floor), two apses and
a barrel-vaulted ceiling... some
historical architectonic recall.
The main sides are opened: one
is the entrance, through the
other you can look at the moon in
changing colours... a path from
reality to imagination. In SL you
can reach the moon but, when
you are there, you'll see that is
only an empty half-sphere, an
illusion. The room's space could
be fitted with different kind of
furniture, a place to meet people,
a place for dancing, a place for
being in love with someone. The
balcony is a flying carpet; on it
there's a flexible shape: you can
sit on it surrounded by the rotating texture of the sky. The pool
is a glass semi-sphere with clear
water; in the centre there is an
iceberg: two physical states, liquid
and solid, in the virtual world.
The tower is a cylinder: in the
centre of the roof there is a big
fire: if you walk in it you fall down
inside. The walls are like melted
metal. It could be a dungeon for
RP. This is the only enclosed
space: you are in it and this is
reinforced by the possibility to
look out through the grate and
transparent ceiling... so high that
you can not reach it...

Beethoven / Ella Fitzgerald ((◀

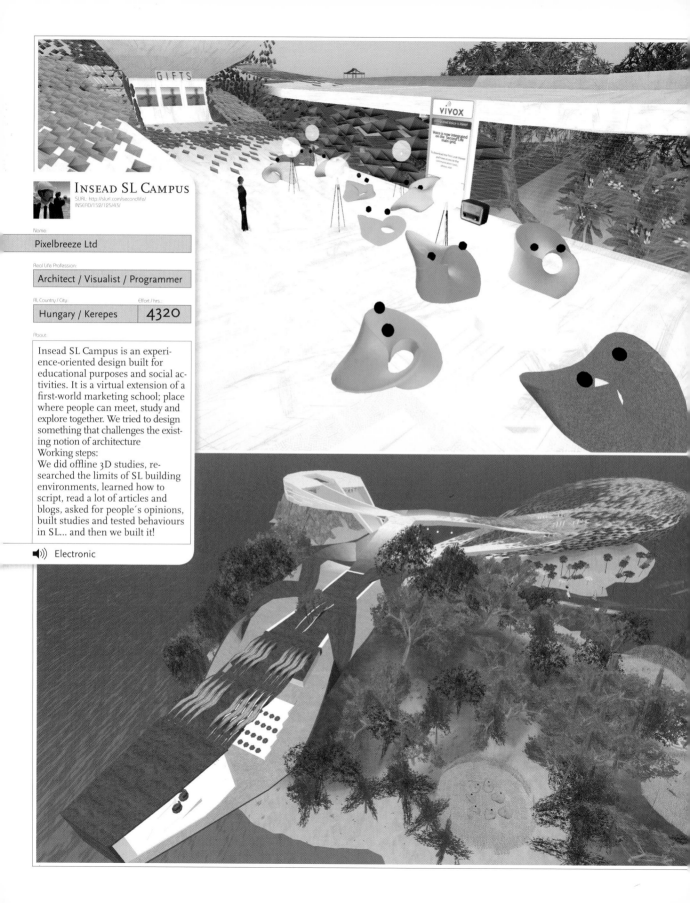

INSEAD SL CAMPUS

SURL: http://slurl.com/secondlife/
INSEAD/152/125/43/

Name:

Pixelbreeze Ltd

Real Life Profession:

Architect / Visualist / Programmer

RL Country / City:

Hungary / Kerepes

Effort / hrs.:

4320

About:

Insead SL Campus is an experience-oriented design built for educational purposes and social activities. It is a virtual extension of a first-world marketing school; place where people can meet, study and explore together. We tried to design something that challenges the existing notion of architecture
Working steps:
We did offline 3D studies, researched the limits of SL building environments, learned how to script, read a lot of articles and blogs, asked for people´s opinions, built studies and tested behaviours in SL... and then we built it!

🔊 Electronic

SCI-FI BUILDING

http://slurl.com/secondlife/Architecture/203/213/23

Name:

Lester Clark aka Designer Dingson

Real Life Profession:

Graphic Designer

RL Country / City:

Surrey, UK

Effort / hrs.:

120

About:

I am a graphic designer in the world's largest residential architecture firm.

This is a freestyle project exploring translucent texturing with a sci-fi feel, bold, strong and striking. Overlapping sounds add to the feel of this exciting build.
I feel strongly that the virtual architects in Second Life need to push at the boundaries of what is possible, with only technology and imagination as the limiting factors; every virtual architect has the duty to deny all convention attached to a real world build scenario.
The virtual architects in Second Life are the emerging prophets of a new age, they are charged with bringing into being radical and visionary works of art.

🔊)) Country to The Prodigy

AIRPORT
SURL: http://slurl.com/secondlife/Klein/239/222/30

Name:

Peter Scharmüller

Real Life Profession:

Media Artist

RL Country / City:

Austria / Vienna

Effort / hrs.

2160

About

It is an airport that works with several architectural layers. The roof is a flight deck where big airplanes can land. the ground-floor is the media presentation center, lobby and office center. The building itself rests at sea-side, with a falling coast. 1st lower level is the airport terminal where passengers wait for their flights. Then the 1st flight deck and a harbour/marina for ships and seaborne helicopters.

Punk Rock

RENDERING SPACE *by Lester Clark (Designer Dingson in Second Life), August 2007*

I'M TRYING TO EXPLAIN "IT" – I've yet to classify "it" in my head – to someone who knows nothing of this world. I suppose I'm finding it hard to classify because it's still so fluid, it's changing by the minute and you can see it evolving into something more mature, more powerful.

The "it" to which I refer is the emergence of virtual architecture, structures of all shapes and sizes formed and shaped by the intriguing characters that inhabit a variety of virtual worlds. My mind drifts, I see a catwalk parade of outlandish clothing and accessories, of stick-thin models that exist in what seems like a parallel universe, and it seems similar somehow... the garments that no one will ever really wear, the work that went into these items being worn for that brief moment on the catwalks of Paris and Rome. What I find similar is that what you see on those catwalks – when you look and think – is more than just an outfit; it's a display of creativity and that's what it's supposed to be, the hat that no one will really wear is amazing purely and simply because it's the product of a creative mind; it's outlandish, it defies convention, it exists as a momentary sculpture and it inspires clothing manufacturers and designers worldwide to create something similar that contains just a little of the spark they've just seen but this time its about something that can be sold and used by real people, leading real lives.

The virtual architects that inhabit these worlds are visionaries, the emerging prophets of a new age. The structures and spaces they create, the hours of work they put into them, the new ways they find to express what they have in their minds – it's intriguing, it's fascinating. And I'm not talking about the people that create a box with a roof, I'm talking about the ones who truly understand the medium in which they create; actually it's more than an understanding, it's a compulsion, a drive to create something different, something exciting, something that doesn't conform to any laws of physics, some virtual place that both exists and doesn't exist, all at the same time. The architects and designers that create these virtual structures give us the chance to experience pure creativity again, an art lost to some of the real-life architects today. There was a time when architects were seen as visionaries, when their input was paramount to creating something amazing, something special. Today, sadly, many architects have simply become part of the process, their involvement and input is controlled by other factors; budget constraints and the need for profit mean that many of the structures that start out as exciting designs are value-engineered by assorted parties and become dull. The finest architects, both real and virtual, those with the passion that you can literally feel when you meet them, are amazing people; they value life and how we live it, they strive to create nice places to live and work, they should be admired and encouraged because they exist solely to impact positively on our lives.

I think sometimes that we have lost the ability to rejoice in architecture, to value it as a fundamental sensory addition to our real everyday world. There was a time where even the gates to a building were works of art, when the columns, door handles, chairs, light switches and ceilings were objects of awe. I worry that today's reality means that most of us grow up constantly travelling through the all-too-familiar faceless urban landscapes where "there is no there there" and that this has dulled our senses somehow and muted our desire for greatness. As someone connected to architecture I wonder sometimes about what our generation will leave for our children; will the children of the future still hark back to the structures created by Le Corbusier, Mr Wright, Mies or the Bauhaus? Will we have contributed enough, apart from the iconic, to add to this timeless collection? And is it not conceivable that maybe some of our legacies on an architectural level will ultimately exist as structures in a virtual world? History has given us so many architectural gems – and yes of course a few are still being created – but we live in a modern world now, in a world of MMC and planners, and codes for sustainable houses, of thermal loss calculations and developers' boxes. I accept that these rules, these conditions, these practices all have their place – but within these boundaries, within the limits of what is deemed architecturally acceptable in this "tick box" world, it's inevitable that the architect's

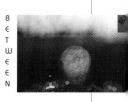

compulsion to bring into being something special will find another route. That compulsion is being played out, in part, with these virtual structures, in the virtual worlds that will become part of all of our lives over the next few years. Ask yourself whether in five years' time we will be scrolling up and down two-dimensional web pages when you go online for information? I guarantee that you will find yourself in a virtual world sooner or later – whether you like it or not, the technology that drives these worlds will inevitably weave itself into the very fabric of our lives.

The responsibility for how these virtual worlds are rendered rests squarely on the shoulders of the designers and architects that populate them, and in a very real sense are helping to "create" them. In one sense, virtual architecture and its disciples must push at the boundaries of what is possible in order to create structures that amaze and inspire. Like the Paris catwalk creators, the challenge here for the virtual architect is to continually learn how to find innovative ways to render space. When there exists such a new world, with only imagination and technology as the limiting factors, then you have a duty to create what is, in this real world, quite impossible. You have a duty to learn how to use the medium of the virtual world to shape your designs and deny all rules and conventions that are attached to structures and buildings in the real world. You are sculptors, tasked with bringing into being radical and visionary works of virtual art.

In another sense, virtual architecture must remain aware of the fact that residential communities are being formed and the halls of virtual corporate business are being laid. In these scenarios one must remain true to the function of the space/place being created; if it's a retail environment then avatars must be able to shop with ease, wayfinding must be intuitive, product selection and trial should be easy and available instantly. The architectural response to these questions is critically important – as a corporate you will only ever truly distinguish yourself in the virtual world by a reliance and insistence upon outstanding creative design, both in exterior form as well as interior design. Corporate institutions need to function effectively in the virtual world, but they need to enter these worlds with an acceptance of a new world order, they need to strive to maximize the client experience on a visual and creative level at all times.

For residential structures it becomes much more an issue of personal taste; if we are to provide a welcome to all those who visit these worlds, we cannot demand of them that they live in a particular style of residence. I see no scenario where creating a traditional family home would be the best answer to the question, and the true architects of this virtual world don't typically engage in this type of building, though it may well be suitable for the person who creates it. In my opinion it doesn't have a lasting place in the future and practice of virtual architecture, but it does surely have a place in the virtual world as someone's home, should they choose it to be so.

The youth of today's mature economies are growing up in a world where digital communication and high-speed internet access are their "norms" – not being able to get online for today's youth would be unthinkable; they expect it, but more importantly to note, they accept it as part of their life. We are a generation that has been given the opportunity to create – and spend time in – fast emerging new worlds. We all have a choice as to what we use these worlds for and how we see these worlds develop. The scope for architectural inspiration, for cross-cultural communication, for educators, for information sharing and globally collaborative events is immense, it's an opportunity that we, collectively, should not squander.

When we move to populate another planet – about which I have no doubt – we will have the very same opportunity again; maybe what we learn about ourselves with the formation of these virtual worlds will inform our decisions about how to tackle building a new real world from scratch. Who knows, if we could learn, in this world, to accept and appreciate the differences between ourselves and our neighbours, in the same way as we are learning to in the virtual ones, we may even find that this real world becomes a nicer place to inhabit.

SECOND LIFE VS. CINEMATIC ARCHITECTURE *by Pascal Schöning, jury member*

SOMEHOW IT SEEMS the world is not ready yet for Second Life. Having watched the first architecture competition, it seems the main intention is to be able to fly, and be everywhere you want in an instant. But then people believe you must land somewhere (like in real life). That is shown in most entries, where the architecture consists of walls, roofs, floors, openings etc., conventional parts of real architecture (like in real life). Only a few contributors were able to switch to memory related items to force interaction. Even those of course used some kind of object – no wonder, because memories are connected to events and physicality (like in real life). The question for me is, how is it possible to create something which functions superior to real life? As long as it offers only a replica it cannot replace real life, where we have philosophy, poetry, visual arts etc., to move into a world of speculation of great dimensions. And there every thing is related to real physicality, the only bit which protects you from going crazy. Even in quantum physics the proof comes only if you can detect something. The means to detect are still related to the human senses and the intellect, but only in relation to real physicality. That is the concept of the cinematic architecture in difference to Second Life.

Maybe I misunderstand Second Life...

Excerpts from the Manifesto of Cinematic Architecture:

THE VERY ESSENCE OF CINEMATIC ARCHITECTURE IS NOTHING LESS THAN THE COMPLETE TRANSFORMATION OF SOLID STATE MATERIALISTIC ARCHITECTURE INTO AN ENERGISED EVER CHANGING PROCESS OF ILLUMINATED AND ENLIGHTENING EVENT APPEARANCES WHERE PAST PRESENT AND FUTURE ACTIVATE A TIME SPATIALITY DEFINED BY THE DURATION PERCEPTIBLE THROUGH OUR SENSES AND STRUCTURED BY OUR MENTAL ABILITY WHERE THE EFFECT OF INDEPENDENT MOVEMENT OF MATTER IN SPACE WHICH IS THE PHYSICAL KINEMATICS IS ITSELF ILLUMINATED BY THE OFTEN CONTRADICTORY REVELATION OF FILMIC CINEMATIC SEQUENCES OF NARRATIVE MEMORY PROCESSES THUS ATTAINING THE OTHERWISE IMPOSSIBLE SIMULTANEITY OF SPACE AND TIME.

(...) To fly into the universe one has to construct a tiny powerful capsule, a concentrated assembly of thousands of well-connected and functioning elements. Only then – and if this capsule is projected by a huge energy-concentration – it is possible to get ejected into the ultimate SPACE. The brain is another compatible concentration of energy-projection. Only the brain (very small in measurable dimensions) allows one to imagine endless space-dimensions (as we know from philosophy, literature, the arts and sciences).

Le Corbusier lived the last years of his life in a small hut (the smaller, original one) on the Cote d'Azur, his cabanon in Cap Martin. He could only sleep in it; it protected him from rain, wind and the cold. But it had a big window in the front towards the sea. From here he could look at the undisturbed surrounding nature, and wide over the water until the curvature of the horizon and the vastness of the sky. And all that after he had dreamed and realized huge material-spaces. He did not need them anymore because the SPATIALITY he envisioned was bigger and constantly changing in its appearance – a cinematic experience. The hut with the big front window open to his universe worked like a movie camera and Le Corbusier's perception and memory as its capturing film stock.

Manifesto for a Cinematic Architecture by Pascal Schöning published by the Architectural Association (http://cinematicarchitecture.com/).

I think that SL is an extension of the RL,
and RL an extension of SL.

IMMAGINARIA

Name:
Arco Rosca aka Paolo Valente / Team

Real Life Profession:
Architect

RL Country / City: Effort / hrs.:
Italy / Rome   640

About

I made this with my team: Olhoblu Ock, Alessandro Biamonti, Urania Wind, Chiara Bond and Ralph Ueltzhoeffer.

Creating a place was this project's main objective. Working within the specific context and limitations presented by SL are the goals to which this proposal aspires. Extending categories such as architecture, town and location in SL is not an easy task, and the perspective from which certain subjects are seen is both elusive and iridescent.

The form in which we propose to comply is the need for stylistic characteristics, staged by the varying "uses and consumptions", and is constructed for the various situations SL presents. A superstructure, a device composed of images and created for the imagination; the primitive cube form in SL becomes the medium for the RL, so that the contemporary man here in SL may further enhance his existence.

It is within this "cube" that the publisher Meltemi finds his way in SL, through its link to the institutional website; but also through the "Director" who communicates directly in SL, whether for publishing a final product or the networking of periodic content.

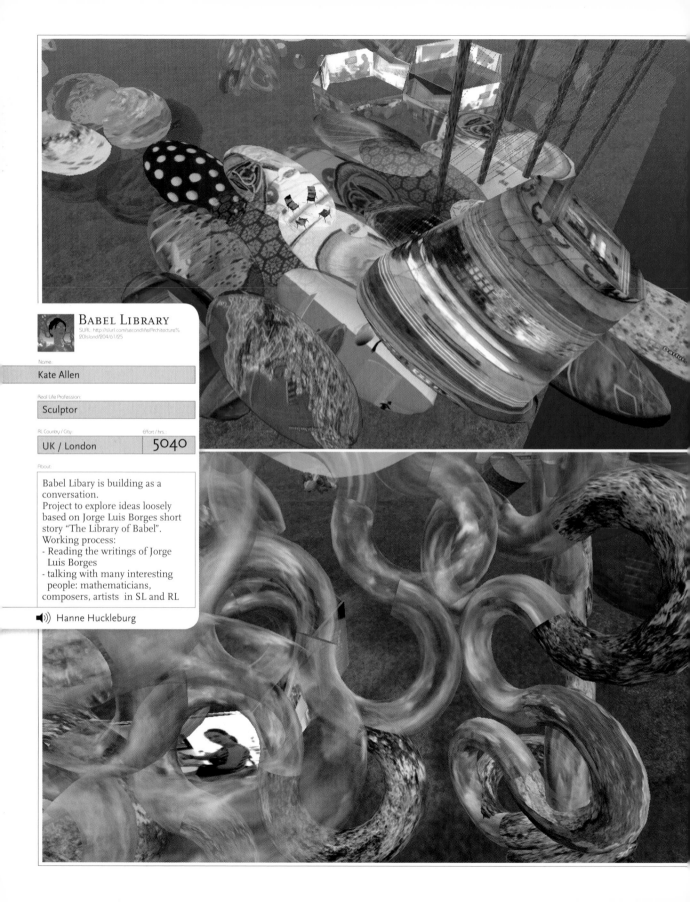

BABEL LIBRARY
SURL: http://slurl.com/secondlife/Architecture%20Island/204/61/25

Name:
Kate Allen

Real Life Profession:
Sculptor

RL Country / City:
UK / London

Effort / hrs.:
5040

About:
Babel Libary is building as a conversation.
Project to explore ideas loosely based on Jorge Luis Borges short story "The Library of Babel".
Working process:
- Reading the writings of Jorge Luis Borges
- talking with many interesting people: mathematicians, composers, artists in SL and RL

◀))) Hanne Huckleburg

All together, as it is, Trash Palace became a vibrant social spot, where people share their lifestyles and music, where friendships emerge as well as love and hate. Without those people, Trash Palace would be nothing more than a bunch of prims.

TRASH PALACE

SURL: http://slurl.com/secondlife/anyMOTION/36/219/241

Name:

Stephan Bolch aka Dave Attenborough

Real Life Profession:

DJ / artist / music producer

RL Country / City: Effort / hrs.:

Germany / Munich   888

About

Trash Palace is an electronic music club in Second Life. We hold live DJ gigs and live music acts and broadcast then via SHOUTcast. It was a factory before, and it morphed into trash. I invited graffiti artists like Van Data to do some of the walls, and met Artoo Magneto who is a really important designer and 3D artist currently working on Trash Palace. Many of the pictures and artworks are my own. I see a lot of creative avatars there, many designers in their own right. I see a mix of styles, which is what I most like: SciFi/Clubwear/Robots/Ballerinas/Fantasy/Cyborgs etc. I really like Richard Rogers. I like all that is deconstructive in a way. In art and music as well. I love to find the structure in the middle of the chaos. I did research in SL for one month, and tried in-world. It is the best you can do as the building is your plan or model. It is a good thing to walk around your building/model and see how it feels and if it has an atmosphere. I never did research in the real world. The last thing I know is that I had been greatly inspired by the Charles de Gaulle airport in Paris. It is organic, old and lives. That is why I love it!

Copying real life is boring! Research! Investigate! Collaborate! Communicate! Build!

Steve Reich / Alban Berg

GALLERY DIABOLUS

SURL: www.slurl.com/ArtGalleryDiabolus (Benvolio), Benvolio (240, 104, 23)

Name:
Noémi Ördög

Real Life Profession:
Architecture Student

RL Country / City:
Austria / Vienna

About:

There are two buildings on the land. One is the Diabolus Virtual Architect Studio. The Architect Studio contains a model workshop, where we build our 1:10 scale models, and a conference room. The second building is the Gallery Diabolus. As there is no gravity in SL we let the building fly in the air, so we have a piazza under the building for special events and projects such as concerts, performances etc. The gallery has two horizontal parts and one vertical, each disappearing in the air at the end. In the horizontal galleries we organise exhibitions for traditional art (photo, painting etc.), the vertical is for special projects. We have a panorama room, a particle emitter workshop and an installation room there. The functional structure of the Gallery:

1. Piazza
2. Audiovisual studio for solid/flexi prim, particles, sound and LSL experiments
3. Diabolus main exhibition space
4. Atelier Verrocchio for group-internal exhibitions and demonstrations
5. Teleport and exhibition information
6. Josina's wearable art (SL fashion design)
7. Stage of the particle emitter theatre (The MANAX synesthesia project)
8. Installation tower to exhibit interactive audiovisual installations and performances.
9. Oldtimer Teleport (elevator)

🔊))) Stravinsky

"SL helps us to get know RL better. We can try new ideas and their functionality."

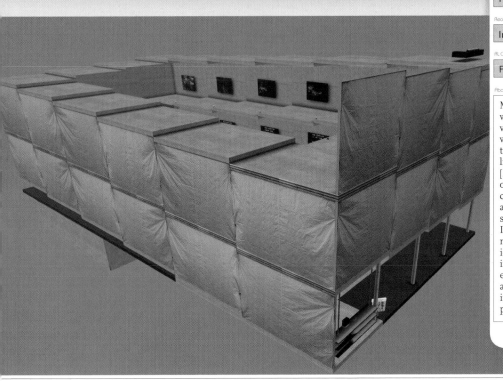

DIGITAL EYES GALLERY
http://sluri.com/secondlife/Kusonagi/198/216/581

Name:

Nadia Clement

Real Life Profession:

International Buyer

RL Country/City: Effort / hrs.:

France / Paris   5376

About

My building is an art gallery in which I tried to make a modern version of classical Arab houses where life revolves around a central patio open to the sky. And this limited by the number of prims. [I was limited by the number of prims.? I limited myself to a certain number of prims.?] From anywhere in the building you can see all the other floors and the art. I like classic architecture and love modern buildings as well, but my ideal would be to see more buildings that don't waste so much energy. I believe that architecture is an art, but not for personal fame; it's more an art to make a pleasant place for people who use it.

MIRROR GARDEN by Mechthild Schmidt Feist (USA / New York)
EduIsland (15, 130, 20)

NEURON COMPLEX by Olaf Finkbeiner (Germany / Frankfurt)
http://slurl.com/secondlife/Professionals%20I/183/162/23/?title=neuron%20complex

UNIVERSITY CAMPUS by International Telematic University
UNINETTUNO (Italy / Rome)
International Telematic University (235, 150, 29)

SECOND LIFE SCHOOL OF ARCHITECTURE
by Ted Mikulski (USA / Enfield)
http://slurl.com/secondlife/architecture%20Island/142/95/27

WORKING PLATFORM FOR UNIVERSITY OF OPORTO STUDENTS
by Paulo Frias (Portugal / Porto)
http://slurl.com/secondlife/Universidade%20do%20Porto/128/128/0

SECONDREIFF by Marc Frohn & Sascha Glasl (USA / Los Angeles)
http://slurl.com/secondlife/UIISE%20secondreiff/165/165/106/
?title=UIISE%20secondreiff&iframe=http%3fi//secondlife.com/

EROTICA by Ibrahim Adelhady (Egypt / Alexandria)

architecture
doesn't only show how
the world can and ought to be;
it actually makes a part
of the world
the way it should be
and is »

« imagination givi
natural pa
to stru

SCAPES by Brad Kligerman & Jamil Mehdaoui / Space (France / Paris)
http://metaverseterritories.com

SIM by PDINSL (Periodic Design in SL), (Japan/ Tokyo)

THE SECOND LIFE OF CLASSIC8 by Alfredo Sabato (Italy / Treviso)
http://slurl.com/secondlife/Architecture/199/145/25

IMPROBABLE ARCHITECTURES by Vera Bighetti, Giselle
Beiguelman, Juliana Constatino & Elaine Santos
(Brazil / Sao Paulo)
http://www.noema.art.br/ai/en/sl.html

DE LODI – VIRTUAL POLAND 1985 by Cezary Ostrowski (Poland / Poznan)
http://slurl.com/secondlife/De%20Lodi/186/19/21/?title=De%20Lodi%20-%20Psychodelic%20Poland&msg=The%20Land%2
0of%20Dreams%20and%20Revolution%20%3A%29

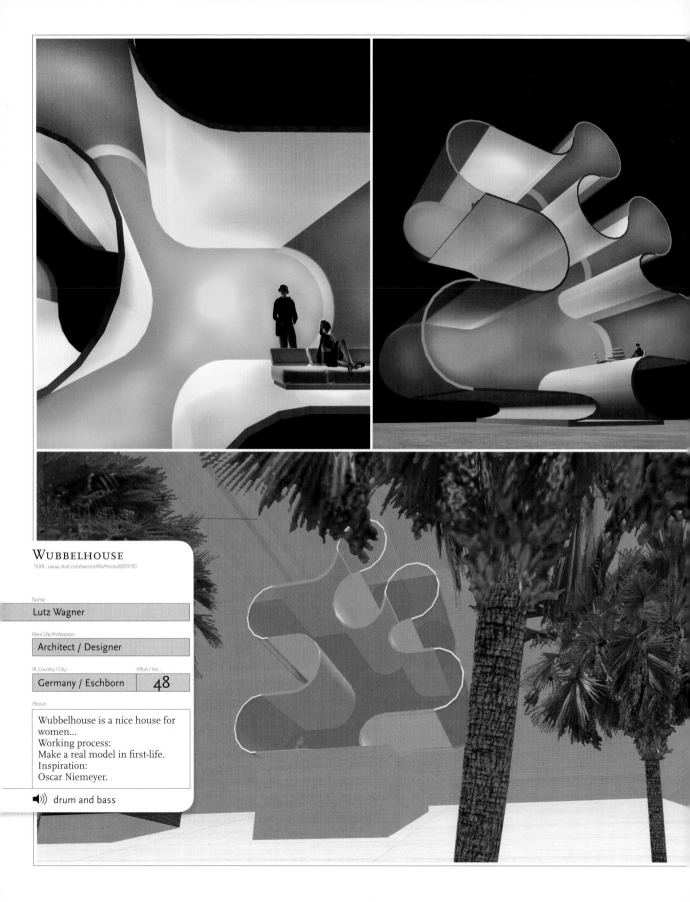

WUBBELHOUSE
SURL: www.slurl.com/secondlife/Hoola/22/9/30

Name:
Lutz Wagner

Real Life Profession:
Architect / Designer

RL Country / City: Effort / hrs.:
Germany / Eschborn   48

About:

Wubbelhouse is a nice house for
women...
Working process:
Make a real model in first-life.
Inspiration:
Oscar Niemeyer.

🔊))) drum and bass

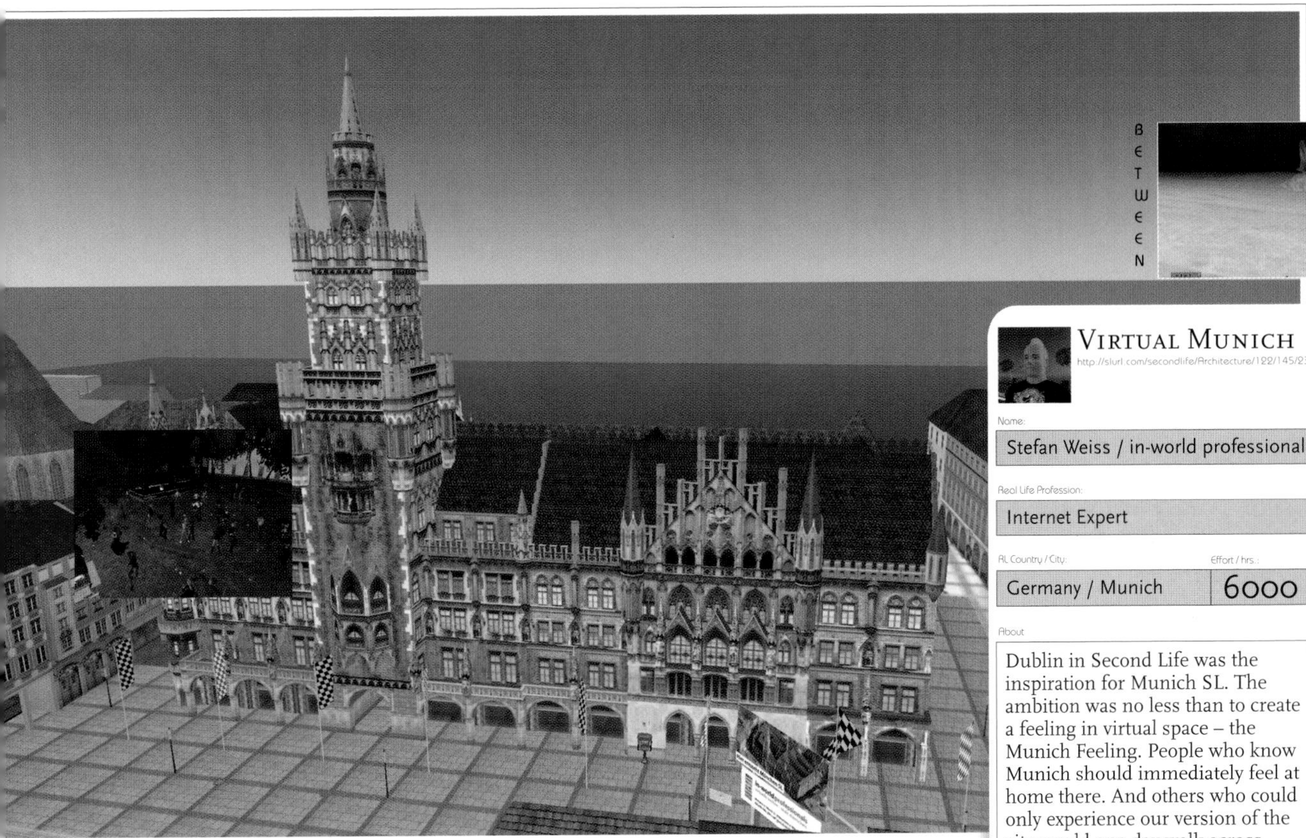

VIRTUAL MUNICH

http://slurl.com/secondlife/Architecture/122/145/23

Name:

Stefan Weiss / in-world professionals

Real Life Profession:

Internet Expert

RL Country / City:

Germany / Munich

Effort / hrs.:

6000

About

Dublin in Second Life was the inspiration for Munich SL. The ambition was no less than to create a feeling in virtual space – the Munich Feeling. People who know Munich should immediately feel at home there. And others who could only experience our version of the city would one day walk across Marienplatz and say, "Hey, this is just like in Second Life." People say we did it.

I am the founder of in-world professionals. The city was built by my developers with my money. That makes me the owner. Owner of a virtual city. On the internet, one would say I'm the community manager. In the virtual world, that makes me the landlord, organiser, publican, friend and helper, curator, guardian of law and order, snow sweeper, best man, silly idiot, host, gardener, event manager – in short, the dogsbody girl. At least it makes me the mayor. I'm not unhappy about it, either.

Preparations for the next big step of virtualisation: GPS-driven mobile media connect the virtual with the real city...

"Speech Bubble", text communication in physical space, mobile installation / performance, Plazes, Berlin and Ars Electronica 2007, by Aram Bartholl.

MIXED REALITIES, ART PROJECTS & PERSONAL EXPERIENCES OF VIRTUAL AND REAL

PEOPLE

"The spectacle is not a collection of images; rather, it is a social relationship between people that is mediated by images. The spectacle cannot be understood either as a deliberate distortion of the visual world or as a product of the technology of the mass dissemination of images. It is far better viewed as a weltanschauung that has been actualized, translated into the material realm – a world view transformed into an objective force."

– GUY DEBORD

The Society of the Spectacle, tr. Donald Nicholson-Smith, New York 1995, p.12–3. First English edition 1970; French original 1967.

ONLINE SYMBOLS IN THE OFFLINE WORLD *by Aram Bartholl*

The data-based world of digital networks has become an increasingly important part of everyday life. A diverse array of platforms, devices and services vie for our attention. In which form does this network-data-world manifest itself in our physical everyday-life space? What is being fed back into physical space from the "cyberspace" into which data has been fed for so long? How do these digital innovations influence our actions in everyday life? For several years now, Aram Bartholl has been working in the field of inquiry delineated by these topics and questions and investigating the feedback effects of general digitization as an approach to gaining an understanding of the technological transformation of society. In the form of objects, installations, interventions, performances and workshops he takes the developments of recent years to the analogue physical space and attempts to get to the bottom of the issues inherent in them.

1 "Map" red marker of the location based search service Google Maps. Public space installation, Berlin 2006

2 "WoW" identity in virtual and physical space. Workshop and performance, Vooruit.be, Gent, Belgium 2007

3 "Speech Bubble" and "Chat", text communication in physical space, mobile installation / performance, Plazes, Berlin and Ars Electronica 2007.

4 "Second City: Bringing Second Life in to public space, blurring the borders of virtual reality and the city". City intervention, several installations, Ars Electronica 2007.
© ARAM BARTHOLL

124

I – BUY – EVERYTHING *by Florian Kuhlmann*

The virtual space of the media and the reality generated by our brain produce a synthetic space where the social life of modern techno-societies is played out. Capital and broadcasting installations have always formed an unholy alliance. Capital controls the installations and thus dominates the synthetic space largely autocratically. But thanks to net-based virtual worlds such as Secondlife.com a new, hitherto inaccessible sphere for the masses has opened up. The I-buy-everything event is a hybrid happening that exploits in particular this phenomenon of opening up. The happening took place partly in Cologne, partly in SL. Guests joined in from all over the world. The indiscriminate purchase of digital artefacts produced by purchasers illustrates the nonsense of an economy based on shortages in virtual space and plays therewith. The picture put together from various parts of the happening and shown both in RL and SL reinforces the impression of the shredding of existing structures.

© COLLAGE BY FLORIAN KUHLMANN

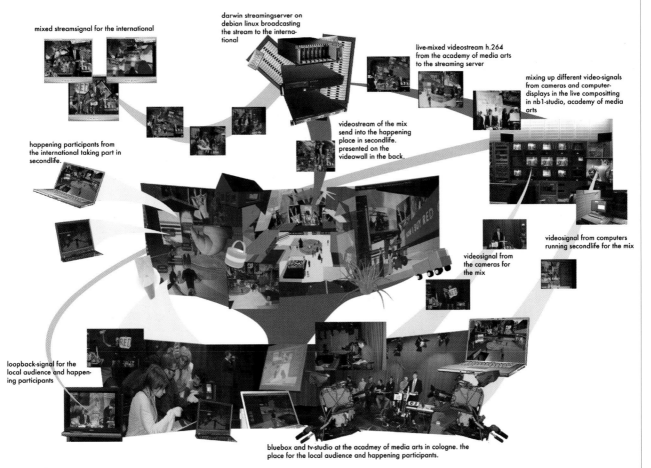

mixed streamsignal for the international

darwin streamingserver on debian linux broadcasting the stream to the international

live-mixed videostream h.264 from the academy of media arts to the streaming server

mixing up different video-signals from cameras and computer-displays in the live compositting in nb1-studio, academy of media arts

videostream of the mix send into the happening place in secondlife. presented on the videowall in the back.

happening participants from the international taking part in secondlife.

videosignal from computers running secondlife for the mix

videosignal from the cameras for the mix

loopback-signal for the local audience and happening participants

bluebox and tv-studio at the acadmey of media arts in cologne. the place for the local audience and happening participants.

AVATAR ORCHESTRA METAVERSE *International Mixed Reality Project, since February 2007*

There is a sort of surreal irony in doing art in an artificial world; it is so obvious that it can only be distinguished in definition. It is only terminology – what you name the thing – that makes the canvas different from the wall it hangs on. In here more than outside both are mere representations, and it is hard to maintain an art versus everything else discourse because the daily routine in Second Life is always already a surreal vision. Everything is by default interactive, audiovisual and ever-changing. Avatars take shape after Marcel Duchamp's nude descending the stairs, blood pours from the sky and the world can at any time turn into a painting by René Magritte.

Second Life adds up to a heterogeneous and complex society, and it can easily be found to be both open-minded and inclusive. A huge stage for a democratic kind of theatre where everyone is at once actor, director and audience. With William Shakespeare we can say that this is not so different from the real world. After all there is more to Second Life than Potemkin villages imitating what we already know in real life. The networking, interaction, cooperation and presence are real qualities of Second Life. Which is also what one needs to found an orchestra.

Originally the Avatar Orchestra Metaverse arose from the need to perform two projects simultaneously, one by Harold Schellinx and the other by Shintaro Miyazaki, or in this world better known as Hars Hefferman and Maximillian Nakamura. The orchestra doesn't have a fixed size, nor will it ever have one. An ever-changing mix of backgrounds and generations shape the orchestra at any given time. What it does have at present is a dedicated core of about fifteen members, to which they also occasionally add guest performers and guest sound installations. To approach the idea of an orchestra in such an elastic manner makes the logistics easier, as the performers are based in Europe, North America and East Asia, with the potential of adding the rest of the world. The orchestra counts among its members programmers, architects, visual, digital and performance artists as well as musicians and all the possible mixed breed. Until recently the compositions, instruments, animations and staging were all made by members of the orchestra, and all these were made with the specific pieces in mind. Always expanding and seeking new ways of using the body of the orchestra, the orchestra has found itself approached by composers from both outside the orchestra itself and outside Second Life, so adding to its scope collaborations with composers of the avant-garde adapting works to this virtual environment.

... this is a real live event

Founding members are *Maximillian Nakamura (SL name) aka Shintaro Miyazaki (Berlin / Germany), Miulew Takahe (SL) aka Björn Eriksson (Stockholm / Sweden), Bingo Onomatopoeia (SL) aka Andreas Müller (Regensburg / Germany), Hars Hefferman + Frans Peterman (SL) aka ookoi (France / Netherlands) and Vit Latynina + Paco Mariani (SL) aka Pomodoro Bolzano (Regensburg / Germany).*

(BASED ON "NEW DIRECTIONS IN MUSIC BY AVATARS" BY LEIF INGE, 2007)

"... the Avatar Orchestra Metaverse approaches Second Life as the instrument itself".

1 When the virtual hits reality. Containers of art occupy the main square in the German town of Regensburg.

2 The real church and its virtual "heaven".

3 The virtual home base, where the "virtu-real" action takes place...

4 Avatar Orchestra performance at the Avastar island during the awards ceremony of the architecture competition in Second Life. The performance was screened live at Zollverein Essen.

© BY THE ARTISTS

1 *The island "public townscape" at its very beginning on July 20, 2007. A blank standard shaped SIM, type 1.*

2 *July 22, 2007: Within hours after opening the island for the public the shape and the ground level has completely changed. The soil is nearly completely claimed. Due to multiple terraforming actions the multifaced buildings are either hovering or sunken.*

© FLORIAN RÜGER

6 *August 15, 2007: The first group meeting of Public Townscape. Residents adopt the implementation of general guidelines, a controlling body called "officers" and the division of the island into four different administrative sectors.*

7 *August 18, 2007: The "restart" of Public Townscape. All buildings and objects have been returned to their owners and residents start to take posession of Public Townscape again.*

8 *October 27, 2007: The residential area: it was decided via group vote that this administrative sector has to stay free of residential buildings on the ground. A public park with several interesting locations has been established since September 2007.*

9 *September 5, 2007: The residential area: Residents are allowed to build private houses (with max 125 prims) in this administrative area above the park 200 meters or higher. Many residents are linking their homes together to huge hovering platforms.*

PUBLIC TOWNSCAPE *by Florian Rüger*

http://slurl.com/secondlife/public%20townscape

"I wanted to become an officer, because without rules I can't exist!"

ONE PARTICIPANT IN THE EXPERIMENT.

I t's an island, it´s free, it´s in development, it has become mostly harmless and it's the experimental outcome of a diploma thesis in the field of landscape architecture. Public Townscape is an attempt to create and develop a public space in Second Life. The actions on the island are completely up to its visitors and residents. Avatars were invited to create their own public space, find their own way to coexist and to develop it. The only guideline is a very basic main issue of a public space: it has to stay free of charge and accessible to everyone. Let anarchy rule and let´s see what happens...!

3 *July 26, 2007: People with military clothes and weapons "conquered" the island. Peaceful Public Townscapers are getting shot. Some residents are leaving the island because of this violent turn.*

4 *August 4, 2007: Nearly all buildings got buried under heaps of earth. Some considered it art, others as a way to upset and expel residents from the island in order to absorb their raw materials, the prims.*

5 *July 28, 2007: Because of the massive terraforming on the ground and the military activities, a lot of residents are moving their objects into higher regions of the island. Several gardens, houses and parks are floating between 200 and 800 meters high.*

P E O P L E

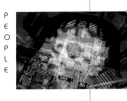

10 *August 26, 2007 @ the special event area: The first public concert on Public Townscape. Ish and Neekie Lednev, two live musicians are inaugurating this administrative sector with smooth jazz.*

11 *September 9, 2007: The special event area: participants of the "1st Annual Architecture & Design Competition in Second Life" are tracking the livestream of the jury decision, that took place at the Ars Electronica Festival in Linz, Austria in this sector of Public Towncape.*

12 *October 27 2007: The special event area: a public Halloween party for all residents of Public Townscape and visitors, organized by the residents and officers.*

13 *October 10, 2007: The townhall area: The townhall was was designed and erected in an open competition among the residents.*

14 *October 27, 2007: The townhall area: Administrative devices in front of the townhall-hill. Prim counter, audio-stream controlling, teleporters, shortcuts to the most interesting locations in Public Towncape can be found there.*

15 *October 27, 2007: The sandbox area: A place where residents and visitors can experiment, build and script without restrictions.*

This area is now cleared completely every two days…

EVERYDAYNESS

— TOR LINDSTRAND

> "We realized that it is rather hard for people to take in too much at the same time. Instead of taking in the chaos and letting go of focus and control, people seem to choose one part of the chaos and concentrate on that."
>
> — *Rocky Horror Crew*

The following is a **self-generated conversation** about the world of Second Life, its possibilities and its flaws. It's a compilation of texts written by students at the School of Architecture at the Royal Institute of Technology in Stockholm, Sweden. It was done as part of a one day event at NADINE Brussels in April 2007. The different texts have been organized into topics concerning different aspects of Second Life. Then the texts are cut into pieces and are redistributed amongst the topics they have created.

The way everything in Second Life is privately owned is an important part of the in-world culture. In short, people tend to be very protective of their possessions (objects, land, avatar). The creation and usage of these objects becomes the purpose of most Second Life activity (other popular activities include: sex, role-playing, sitting in chairs, conversations, sex and... Oh, did I mention sex?). **The first impression of Second Life could roughly be described as MTV gone wild, with people looking like Beyonce and living like Beyonce. Except they have bigger breasts and a much bigger TV.** ALL IMAGES © TOR LINDSTRAND, LOI ARCHITECTS

"It is getting harder than ever to tell where reality stops and SL begins."
— *Gunnar Lindstedt*

"The virus architecture consists of a space-producing bracelet, providing free architecture and a solution for avatars who want to change the world without owning it."
— *Moa Andrén*

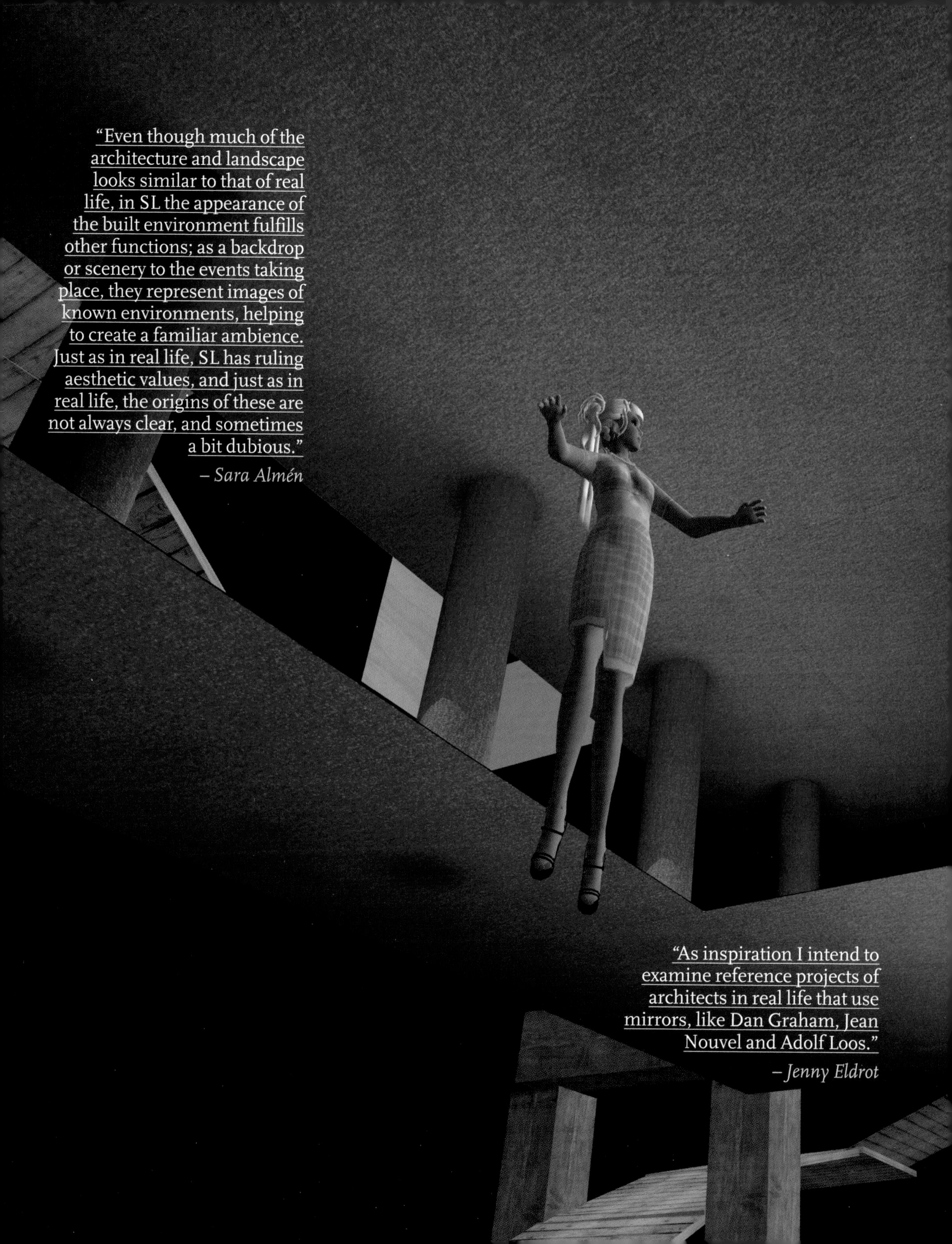

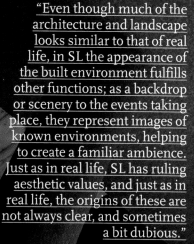

"Even though much of the architecture and landscape looks similar to that of real life, in SL the appearance of the built environment fulfills other functions; as a backdrop or scenery to the events taking place, they represent images of known environments, helping to create a familiar ambience. Just as in real life, SL has ruling aesthetic values, and just as in real life, the origins of these are not always clear, and sometimes a bit dubious."

– Sara Almén

"As inspiration I intend to examine reference projects of architects in real life that use mirrors, like Dan Graham, Jean Nouvel and Adolf Loos."

– Jenny Eldrot

ARCHITECTURAL
REPRESENTATION WITHIN
SECOND LIFE

"Even though a new type of system of structuring space is needed it is still real life people who use SL and we need real life symbols to understand a situation. In a world without limitations like gravity, climate, basic needs for food and sleep, where you can fly as well as walk and teleport your self wherever, more then anywhere this is a place where we need to use traditional symbols to know how to interact."

– Sanna Ridderstolpe/
Jessica Strandell

In a world where the production of desire has been completely overtaken by market economy the major influence in thinking about architecture is more about other media than through architecture itself. This is something that clearly manifests in the platform Second Life. Rather than spatial experiences, it is much more about images, television, movies and games. The image of space in virtual worlds have a direct relation to how the image of architecture is becoming more and more dominant in contemporary architecture, how we consume architecture as much through Hollywood, expensive coffee table books and tourist information as we do through actually being in space. This could also work as an explanation why in user created virtual worlds, where you can do whatever you want design becomes so mainstream and totally predictable. Modelled more on the television show MTV Cribs, another example of design done by people who can do whatever they want, than any critical concepts of space.

Before the Renaissance, which saw the invention of the linear perspective, spatial experience was detached from imagery. Earlier images proposed relations to human activity, symbols of power and emotional reflections. The experience of space was confined within the specific practice of building. Architecture was media specific. With the tools to depict three dimensional space onto a two dimensional surface, architecture and the understanding of space leaped into a new era. The possibility for a viewer to imagine him/herself walking around inside an image opened up a whole new chapter in art, as well as a fundamental shift in the experience of space. The genre Capriccio, to paint representations of architecture in idealist settings was the first step towards the representation of architectural ideas that computer programs have become so fluent in creating. At the same time it introduced the notion of virtuality, of something that is not real but could contain the properties of the real. This duality or split between the real and the representation of the real or the representation of objects as we see them and their measured description, have been unwittingly, in many respects, mutually determined and transformed.

Unfortunately the opportunities that are embedded in the virtual, as a state of pure potentiality, are often quickly brushed aside in favour of technical prowess and over-simplified capitalist strategies. Rather than critically questioning the relations between virtuality and actualisation, images promote the on-going spectacularisation of space.

On-line platforms, as such, are not breaking down any conventions, but they can help us to see things differently. Maybe even think differently. Following the thinking of French sociologist Bruno Latour; it's not so much about changing things by doing the opposite, which is more like producing an image in a mirror while continuing to do the same. It is much more about changing the way things change.

A computer program like Excel has had a greater impact on contemporary architecture than all star architects have managed together. When economy and architectural concepts become increasingly intertwined and opaque then the traditional role of the architect transforms and opens up decision making for professions traditionally remote from the design process. In virtual worlds it paradoxically becomes possible to look beyond architecture as representation and instead discuss these underlying structures of architectural production. A place where we can re-think social concepts, work, life and networks and a possibility to stop thinking about what architecture looks like and start to engage in what architecture does.

"The representation of form in SL is what you might see as only textures, impressions and no function. The appearance of the representation of objects and space is recognizable to us from real life. You find normal houses with a kitchen and a toilet, beautiful garden or a sand beach and a sail boat. The behaviour of the representation is freer than real life since it can lose gravity, become non-solid and objects can respond and act by a script."

– *Sanna Ridderstolpe/ Jessica Strandell*

"A great possibility of the virtual architecture is the possibility of rapid change."
— *Moa Andrén*

"The result is often not what you would wish for, and most times these directly transferred buildings are a real disaster to experience for your avatar."
— *Studio Unreal*

OBJECT CREATION, GENERATION AND INTERACTION

The way mainstream media reports about the phenomena of online worlds very often inscribe them in a clear divide between virtual and real. This separation is somewhat problematic - it's something that has been adopted from literature, especially science-fiction, a fantasy about parallel universes. Furthermore it is always only mentioned in relation to 3D worlds, no one really talks about being immersed in chat rooms or whilst browsing. Since text based experiences haven't been popularly inscribed into the idea of a Cyberspace or a Metaverse it has avoided some of the simplifications attached to the preconceived understandings of 3D environments. When it comes to architecture there are much greater differences between being an architect today compared to the 1930's, than there is between real and virtual architecture. Working with architecture in virtual worlds means that we have to research their specific properties, how they are constructed, what are the concepts of site and subjects. In Second Life the avatar has a humanoid physical representation that flies and has unique ways of looking, a kind of 100 meter radius 360-vision. This disconnects with the way representation is manifested and actual properties pose enormous problems when it comes to architecture. It is not until we fully understand these relationships and how they operate that we can produce something that is really interesting. When architecture becomes more specific in relation to how we actually experience things, maybe then, we will see a completely new kind of architecture. But this means we will have to re-think almost everything we know of architecture, which is so grounded in how we are in and the physical limitations of this world.

Q&A

SD: Would you think that computer games or virtual worlds in general change our sense of orientation?
TL: The notion of the virtual are often interpreted as a notion of a world parallel to reality, this more technological approach are frequently used as a fictional device propelling stories in movies, books and also computer games. It is also one explanation to why games like Second Life often are considered boring and lifeless, it does not live up to the expectations derived from the literature it is being built upon. In this sense I believe that the impact of computer games on the experience of actual, physical space is limited. However the profound effect that we live our lives in an accelerating rate through media is something that clearly changes our perspective and understanding of the reality around us. The virtual, rather than being a clear manifestation that we can model our reality around, is like an undercurrent pushing ideas, concepts and knowledge towards the surface.

Would you think that computer games or virtual worlds in general change our relation between people - and if so in which way? What role does physical architecture play in that "game"
Historical built environments are still the main source of experience in games and virtual worlds. The dived between mediated space and actual space has been about for hundreds of years but it still seems like we struggle with ideological issues surrounding authenticity and truth. Architects and game producers alike are still trying to reconnect the relation between representation and actual, even though they do so from fundamentally different positions. As long as this struggle continue I guess we have to live our virtual worlds in medevil misch-masch and our real life in environments of faux slick-pure.

What is your vision of the architecture of the 21st century (say the next 50 years)?
With so many more professions being engaged in design practice, I foresee a further blurring of distinctions and a further mediation of space. Unfortunately architects will become more and more defensive, backing into a position where they reduce their practice to a designer of costumes for buildings, rather than to take on the struggle for the possibilities to engage in the political and structural side of the production of space.

"The virtual online platform has a range of possibilities that could enrich a production in First Life."
— *MDT*

"Regarding the actual meeting of worlds: the physical world has such a strong presence that the virtual world always becomes something secondary. With the experiment of an event simultaneously in two worlds the actual event taking place in front of you will always produce the strongest experience."

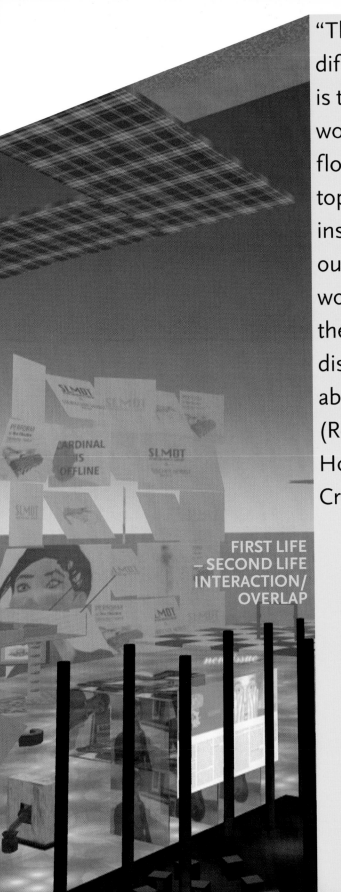

"The difference is that this world is floating on top of and inside of our own world with the physical distances abolished." (Rocky Horror Crew)

FIRST LIFE
– SECOND LIFE
INTERACTION/
OVERLAP

HOW GREEN IS YOUR SPACE?

– KATE ALLEN

"The essence of architecture is the space between people and its construction, and Second Life shrinks, alters and extends this space."

– *Avatar Doesi Beck*

The idea to hold meetings in *Second Life* developed in discussion with research group Performance in Transit, including mathematician Marcus du Sautoy, composer Dorothy Ker, choreographer Carol Brown and myself. We had had several meetings funded by the Gulbenkian Foundation and the AHRC, all at different locations in the UK. When the site of the next meeting was being discussed a virtual meeting in Second Life was suggested. This was conceived both in relation to practical considerations, that is, the problems of organising meetings between geographically dispersed participants, and as a way of exploring the various ideas and performances of multidimensional and virtual space.

I proposed the research group's meeting place in Second Life as a project for RIBA Architecture Week 2007, as the theme was "How green is your space?" exploring ecological buildings. I thought it would be interesting to discover if Second Life could be considered as a green space for meetings and I proposed a meeting occurring in Second Life, with a live webcast in the real world. The Design Museum saw the potential of having a simultaneous virtual and real-life meeting and offered to host the events in their café. The speakers who

all gave their time for free were: Doesi Beck (Germany), Alfredo Desideri (Italy), Keystone Bouchard (USA), Kapitol Metropolitan (Sweden), Designer Dingson (UK), Chip Poutine (Canada) and Scope Cleaver (USA). Some of the texts from the Second Life discussions were projected onto the outside wall of the Design Museum in London at night creating another dimension to the meetings and the discussion. The projected texts were sent via mobile phone messages – the text number was also advertised to the public for one night to text their responses to the Architecture Week theme "How green is your space?"

Composer Dorothy Ker asked me to install text into six floating spheres in an inlet the shape of a question mark (inspired by Borges[1]) so she could play them in a similar way to an instrument during the discussion. The texts created a space that was quite chaotic with the discussion being punctuated by the many different versions of texts often repeating, sometimes creating accidental sense. I built a version of The Klein Bottle,[2] an object that can only be experienced in the fourth dimension, a finite but unbounded space, as is the universe and is the revelation in the story of the "Library of Babel" that the library is finite but unbounded. I hoped the objects built for the meeting would provide keys to start different conversations that the research group had discussed.

Keystone Bouchard gave two talks, one about using Second Life to visualise architecture and the other about the Wikitecture experiment where multiple contributors co-create a design. Keystone emphasised from the outset that building a community, sharing and collaborating were some of the most important aspects of Second Life and that it was through community engagement with the various architectural groups in Second Life that had accelerated his learning curve. Keystone's introduction into Second Life was through his ecological design residential architecture practice, which worked across a wide geographical area. He saw the possibility of using Second Life, because of its ubiquity and ease of use, to

hold meetings with long distance clients. Also important was the ability to walk his clients through schematic design ideas which he found much more immersive and engaging than sending two-dimensional PDF drawings by email. The building tools in Second Life may not be as extensive as some modelling programmes but are good for visualising the general concepts of an idea and can allow the client to test paint colours, furniture layouts, landscaping options etc.

Keystone gave a general overview of building techniques in Second Life and described how real-life architects are using Second Life as a visualisation tool. He explained how architects can build a design concept and test it out by inviting others to explore it and provide feedback, and he mentioned the aLoft hotel as an example. This was a full-scale replica of a hotel design soon to be built in real life in several destinations. The feedback provided by avatars in Second Life was used to revise parts of the design before it was built in real life. Keystone also saw further potential for architects where Second Life buildings could act as a virtual augmentation of a real building, for example a conference centre where virtual conferences are held to compliment real-life conferences. Big companies such as IBM already use Second Life for meetings.

Keystone then described the other opportunity for architects in Second Life to consider building for the virtual environment. He felt that architects should lead the way as to how the two worlds interface and overlap. In response to a question from avatar Bjorlyn Loon about whether the architectural community was beginning to catalogue some of the differences between real life and Second Life builds and find ways to address the differences, the general feeling was that although individual members are starting to discuss these issues such as Chip Poutine's Virtual Suburbia blog, (www.virtualsuburbia.com), there needs to be a lot more discussion. Keystone said that a new language for virtual architecture was needed. Far Link agreed, suggesting the need for a new "5points" manifesto for virtual design.

Scope Cleaver is an avatar working with virtual architecture and design – he had just joined forces with designer Maximilian Milosz and gave a tour of their new store selling furniture and designing buildings in Second Life. Scope gave an interesting talk describing his creative process which was very painterly, starting with creating a colour palette. Unlike Keystone's descriptions of working from plans Scope described a more intuitive freestyle approach to building with lots of trial and error, but using a great deal of control over his textures and the composition of the build, describing how he tries to make the building "photogenic" from certain angles, which also dictated where the vegetation would go.

YOU:
So being in Second Life means I am in front of my computer, I feel the sun on a beautiful afternoon in Munich. At the same time I am here with you...

MARJORIE MILES:
Being able to occupy multiple spaces sets interesting potential

FAR LINK:
It seems to me to be a question of inhabitation versus occupation.

YOU:
I didn't have any better term than "Bastard Space" to describe that.

IOTA ULTSCH:
Lol

FAR LINK:
Nice

MACH VOLITANT:
Far – what do you mean by that?

MARJORIE MILES:
I like that term. It suggests a hybrid space. I'm interested in where people choose to be online and how they chose to define that space with architecture.

FAR LINK:
Occupation being a physical displacement by the body versus a notion of a mental inhabitation (more having to do with attention and the ability to interact with an environment)...

KEYSTONE BOUCHARD:
in a sense, it is the ultimate
in sustainable design

KEYSTONE BOUCHARD:
for example, if we could
somehow measure the
demographics of the
people viewing this event
right now...

KEYSTONE BOUCHARD:
and consider the
environmental footprint
it would require to get us
all, physically in the same
room.

KEYSTONE BOUCHARD:
of course, the servers
consume energy, and your
computer is consuming
energy – but as virtual
environments become
increasingly viable and
easy to use – it is not
unreasonable to expect
that it will be able to
replace certain kinds of
physical architecture.

KEYSTONE BOUCHARD:
and if that's possible
– I think architects should
be thought leaders in
determing how the two
worlds interface and
overlap.

Lecturer of art history Alfredo Desideri felt it was important that new architecture must be informed by architectural history and this influenced his building in Second Life. During his tour he described how Palladio had based his work on the teaching of Vitruvio and that he lived during a period of experimentation. Alfredo said that Le Corbusier had taken Palladio's rules and modified them to create his work; Alfredo's challenge was to modify these rules to make buildings that would fit with the mind avatar "as behind every avatar is a man or woman". A memorable moment of Alfredo's tour was his building scripted to turn us all into classical statues.

Conversation and collaboration led Theory Shaw and Keystone Bouchard to develop the idea of Wikitecture, which experimented with communal building in Second Life, providing a catalyst for an ongoing discussion about co-creating and collaboration in virtual worlds. Second Life allows you to choose who can modify your objects and you can set up a group to do this. The project is still in development, creating lots of discussion; Chip Poutine described it as a kind of architectural jazz. The first experiment highlighted several issues that needed to be worked out before the next wikibuild, such as a good method of automatically recording changes to the build and some kind of voting mechanism. Chip Poutine pointed out a fundamental problem with the wikibuild idea, using the example of Wikipedia where the discussion forms around sources and research to gain a consensus toward an objective fact, whereas in matters of architectural design the discussion is much more subjective. This led to a discussion about value and leadership and whether a collaborative build leads to the lowest common denominator? There was a sense in the discussion that the ease of changing and erasing buildings in Second Life would prevent this, and in a way Second Life is a group of personal wikis constantly changing building conversations.

A topic that came up in several discussions was why much of the architecture in Second Life was built to replicate architecture in the real world and why is it often quite boring? How is form being generated when there are no functional or economic limits? Chip Poutine noted that the pastoral landscape of Second Life creates a certain kind of response; that we just drag in our baggage of what we think architecture should look like; about the difference between making computer games where the space created in the computer was not only a representation of something to be built in the real world but rather an architectural artefact in and of itself. Second Life encompasses both ends of the spectrum: as Far Link put it, "I see it working along a scale at one end mimicking reality and at the other a fantastic exploration."

Keystone felt that taking cues from real life is an important step in the transference between worlds. Design primes the viewer into a particular kind of mindset that informs the dialogue and interaction within the space.

Second Life can give you the opportunity to live a lifestyle that far exceeds your real-life possibilities. Second Life can be used to build virtual copies of real-life buildings and showcase clients' projects. Designer Dingson bought a copy of the Farnsworth House created by Maximilian Milosz to share his interest and admiration for Mies Van de Rohe with the rest of the world and to inspire us to visit the real building.

He describes how the building works well in the perfect world of Second Life where the sharp edge of modernism cannot be blunted by time and the elements. In his talk he wondered if

"According to calculations by Julian Bleecker, each avatar generates a carbon footprint equal to that of driving an SUV 1293 miles."
— *Patrick Lichty*

"It is a kind of
architectural jazz."
– *Avatar Chip Poutine*

owning the virtual house rather than having to live in the real version was more enjoyable, as the real-life upkeep, the leaves staining the decks, the threat of flooding, the bugs at night, the ventilation etc., distracted from the beauty and simplicity of the house. Designer Dingson created a series of easels in the grounds of the Farnsworth House, which set out the history and design of the house. The talk was given in collaboration with Chip Poutine who spoke from a personal perspective charting his interest in the idea of Virtual Architecture since the mid-1990s, waiting until a virtual environment arrived that could allow his ideas to be fulfilled. Chip described his idea to create a memory space – a contemporary digital manifestation for a classic mnemonic device used by orators to deliver speeches over two hours long without the use of notes. The project remained theoretical in the mid-1990s as a feasible technology platform, for the project did not yet exist. Chip joined Second Life in 2005 realising it had the potential to be the kind of space he had been waiting ten years for, where he started writing about the architecture in Second Life and began his virtual architectural practice.

In conclusion, Second Life can be a teaching tool in how to inhabit virtual space.

The essentially ephemeral nature of building in Second Life creates a perfect laboratory environment for art and architecture, to try out ideas for interactive multimedia, interactive scripted objects etc. – for example the walls of an Second Life building could fluctuate in response to a share price going up or down in the real world. These experiments can be tried out easily and at a fraction of the real world cost. The visual nature of the discussion in Second Life helps to understand difficult concepts, as does the possibility for collaboration and sharing ideas and information.

1 Jorge Luis Borges, Fictions, London 1985, John Calder Publishers Ltd.
2 http://www.kleinbottle.com/whats_a_klein_bottle.htm
Page 140: Mobile phone sms 3d projected text, developed with Adrian Haffegee at the
University of Readings Centre for Advanced Computing and Emerging Technologies (ACET)

"Architecture has always existed in a cloud of fantasy, historically the cloud has been mostly literary."
— *Avatar Taliesin Balhaus*

ART IN SECOND LIFE

– MELINDA RACKHAM & CHRISTIAN MCCREA

Email Invaders built by SL artist Annabeth Robinson. SCREENSHOT BY ANNABETH ROBINSON

THE ARRIVAL

A wave rushes and folds neatly on origami shoals. A spotted sky sputters into indecisive clarity. Land pops. Land rises. Lines rush out like ribbons. Names, then faces, then bodies and clothes. Bit by bit, the elements drop into place. Our tour will begin in five minutes. Lives are spent in search of other lives, alternatives for our selves and the indiscreet other voices standing on the edge of the void. Here on the beach before the tour beings pop out of the ether, arriving through their magical invitation. Hello, you. Hello, you. Is that so-and-so? Great tail, where did you get that frock? Linden Labs' desire to have a place for "everybody" really touches the core of the organisation of Second Life, but the actuality is that not everybody is interested. However, the everybody of Second Life is the body of the every. Types and characters, personas and people iterate and shift unlike anywhere and anywhen else in virtual history. The identikit Ikea catalogue of Second Life's personality and appearance matrices are as much about their mutability as their oddity.

As the guests arrive for the tour, appearances shift as characters pose like dolls being undressed by unseen children. Many are unsure, and yet to decide how they will appear, even after they redraw, for this new event. Tonight's tour is an experiment in critically engaging with the creative projects, performances and potentials of Second Life artistic practice, organised for The Good the Bad and the Ugly -empyre- discussion forum.

BEARING WITNESS

Those in our pony tour group who have visited before help the newer, less experienced members to observe proper Second Life etiquette and to ride their ponies correctly. Some stragglers have reconstituted outside the Odyssey building and are battering walls with their fresh new avatar bodies; others are flying around the ceiling. Some have gone exploring and are now submerged underwater wondering why they can still breathe, and others are roaming through Second Life's vast and vacant architectural spaces.

A certain self-consciousness rustles through our crowd and several disappear to redress what they feel are visual inadequacies or inappropriate choices for today's activity. First life galleries don't sell cosmetic surgery and punk haircuts – more's the pity – but here everybody checks their dress code after the birth from the never-never land of their computer's memory buffer. Avatars reappear in different genders and colour schemes, with wings, tails and some delightful new frocks. The sparks of friendships and intimacy are igniting as inventory items are generously shared by those eager to learn and eager to teach.

Spaces like Odyssey provide performing and exhibiting artists an environment in which to ask fundamental questions about art, culture, entertainment and the nature of reality. Most do not see this environment as a simulation of another, external physical space – rather their work seeks to engage with the native attributes of coded environments.

Here the individual ethereal, plasmic, aural and physical body is conjoined with the persistent electronic body of the avatar. We feel his/her feelings, react to his/her stimuli – as aware of his/her in-world presence as we would be of a phantom amputated limb. We have come a long way from the base-camp of well-trodden writings on alterity, and the otherness explored through the early days and MUDs and MOOs. We are collective, we are all queer, we have melded. Our quest[ion]s are different, our entertainment reflects this. But we have mused for far too long and need sustaining engagement.

Seizing the opportunity to try one of Babeli's works Marina Regina jumps onto the harmless looking red plastic chair which is mounted on the large orange painting *Avatar on Canvas*. Nothing seems to happen... then the cohesion of her body disintegrates. She is both stretched

"What I have observed in entertainment forms... is that society is observing itself more. People are able to observe each other on the Net, able to observe each other interact in Second Life and able to observe each other in the second-order artworks that are created to communicate highly personalized interactive works."
– *Christy Dena*

Our tour will begin in two minutes. We mount our pink, blue or yellow steads and teleport to Odyssey.
SCREENSHOT BY ANGELA THOMAS

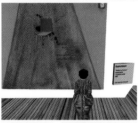

Avatar on Canvas Gazeria Babeli with Marina Regina interacting.

"Visiting Gazira Babeli's retrospective exhibition *Collateral Damage* is a bit like entering an Alice in Wonderland world, simultaneously magical and uncanny. Describing herself as a 'code performer' Babeli makes use of the elastic virtual physics of the digital terrain to create interactive art works where audience interaction sets off a series of playful, unpredictable and sometimes disturbing animations. Her Andy Warhol-inspired work *Second Soup* traps your avatar in a looped animation within the soup can ('You love pop art but pop art hates you!' the work tells you). Another work, *Come Together* enables audience avatars to morph and merge into a collective living sculpture."
- Kathy Cleland

© Screenshots by Melinda Rackham

and squished, her limbs attached in oddly unfamiliar patterns, distorted, deformed, and scratching uncontrollably... Marina still walks and talks and she is clearly unconcerned about a return to normalcy. In fact she seems to enjoy enforced shape shifting!

Our avatars, our new breed of golden code, our selves are held, gently cupped, by their networks, by memories, by fantasy, by potentialities. As the tightly knit pattern unravels, they do not disintegrate depleted, but form other associations. New threads and strings emerge, electronic mucous spans the gaps between, glittering in the orange intensity of a Second Life sunset.

A series of bodies gathers wherever they can; to merely meet people is its own artform in the endless vacant lot. All appearances are deviances in the truest sense; triggers and toggles from central values on a series of scales. As the tour progresses, eyes dart across the polygon mesh. Borders have melted between the group but remnants of collective anxiety are still telepathically cast between species.

PERSISTENCE

> *Time is the medium we live in...*
> *...*
> *...*
> *...to surrender to something*
> *is a feeling which we want to have."*
> Brian Eno

While Brian Eno was addressing the North American premiere of *77 Million Paintings* at San Francisco's Yerba Buena Center for the Arts, four Second Life versions of *77 Million Paintings* were concurrently entertaining in-world fans. Built by Second Life artist Annabeth Robinson and placed across four art venues, each installation was unique, streaming generative sounds, and offering Eno "extras".

Building versions of off-world installations is not Robinson's usual operating mode, rather she addresses the complaint that Second Life is a lonely desolate experience. The majority of her art works require playful participation (whether known or unknown) of avatars to animate them. This interaction may be by touch, collision or chat, or more subtly by surveillance where the artwork scans for avatars in close proximity, pulls data from them, then generates a visual or sonic event.

An early work, *Email Invaders*, requires that the audience send an email to either red or yellow space invaders, which will change size on a towering glass wall, dependant on the length of the email. This methodology of utilising elegantly simple work within the walls of Second Life scripting language overcomes its well-documented narrow parameters. She refers to her working space – The Pencil Factory at the Port – as a sketchbook rather than a studio.

Second life is a persistent medium, so rather than operating within a static technological or art-historical context, this work and other works are always functioning, always "on". The gallery doors to not shut at six PM. The projectors do not turn off.

Robinson's visual metaphor for this constant consumption, for the fragility of self in a persistently present world, is ironically titled *You Demand Too Much of Me*. This sensor/time-based sculpture decays in direct relationship to it's audience numbers – to how much it is on display, looked at, surveilled. More avatars present means the sculpture will disappear, block

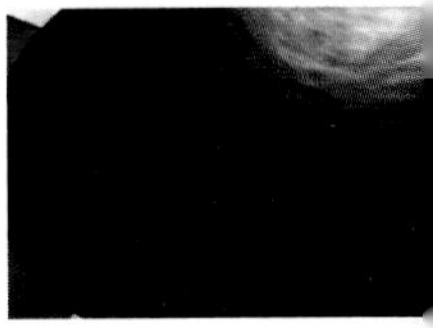

"Simulations only offer
an abstraction of situations,
not of reality."
– *Christian McCrea*

"Does morphic resonance
happen in Second Life
as the formless cohesive
element? Can an avatar have
DNA? Complexity looks at
interacting elements and
asks how they form patterns
and how the patterns unfold,
patterns [that] may never be
finished [because] they're
open ended."
– *Jacquie Clarke*

"In digitized social
networks there is no place
for psychologically defined
notions of personality as a
cohesive, definable whole.
Identity manifests through
notational distributions found
in multiple profiles across
various platforms...
For these articulated identities
[now known as versionals]
connection is the vital point
of communication; not the
content, not the geophysical
inflection, not the biologically-
saturated ties linked to
survival, competition,
and traditional concrete
community building."
– *Netwurker Mez*

While Brian Eno was addressing the North American Premiere of *77 Million Paintings* at San Francisco's Yerba Buena Center for the Arts, four Second Life versions of *77 Million Paintings* were concurrently entertaining in-world fans. Built by SL artist Annabeth Robinson and placed across four art venues, each installation was unique, streaming generative sounds and offering Eno "extras".

© Screenshot by Annabeth Robinson

77 Million Paintings was done under a blueair.tv and Long Now initiative.

The Gate is an evolution of Rodin's *Gates of Hell*
© S꜀ʀᴇᴇɴꜱʜᴏᴛ ʙʏ Rɪᴄʜᴀʀᴅᴏ Pᴇᴀᴄʜ

"For artwork, the possibilities are enormous. I also enjoy the empty spaces. It feels like a dream or like a post-plague society. The structures remain intact. You can go into most places, but you don't own them. You don't have to socialize. This is what initially drew me into Second Life. For the first 3 or 4 months, I had no friends and would walk around and explore. I saw desire embedded in infinite real estate – a sort of extension of Los Angeles."

– *Scott Kildall*

by block, until it is non-existent. Then when there is nothing to look at any more and it is left alone, it slowly reappears one block at a time, like a depleted Terminator reconstituting itself until whole, only to disappear again.

Like Adam Nash, Robinson is pushing the parameters of live in-world generated music and visuals. Her *Avatar Harp* sound installation creates tones when an avatar or other physical object moves within its physical space. Flying through the work, the tones raise in pitch closer to the centre.

While Robinson's works resonates between walls, inside the gallery space, in clearly defined art arenas, Nash's works are more al fresco, venturing into the vast often-derided open public spaces of Second Life. Embedding his poetic, reactive responsive works in Second Life ground gives them an element of accessibility. The park environment – a commons free of perverse advertising and not adverse to instigating queer moments – returns art to the domain of people.

While buildings in Second Life can possess an air of the possessed, the open land between buildings are not the facsimiles of landscape art, but enable the planting of flowers of doubt and surprise. Adam's sonic poems free flow like the art of perpetual, uninterrupted movement, adapting motion to obstacles in the environment. The fluidity of the electro-plasmic body, the gaps and chasms between us, and between us and art are momentarily bridged in-world, in these temporal zones. We flock and swarm between spaces, around spaces, we are dynamic space.

THE GARDEN OF ERRORS

Simulations only offer an abstraction of situations, not of reality. In turn, situations, already abstract, are built entirely out of our expectations and needs. Not every race is thrilling. Not every city is riddled with crime. Simulation is stained with aesthetics.

Artist and curator Marguerite Charmante discusses the layer building in an essay on Second Life in the *Ludic Society Magazine* which connects it to literary ideas of fantasy worlds from Karl Popper, Jorge Luis Borges and others:

> "Second Life remains attractive as a set of rules (a game?), a willfully taken constraint, a bondage. Like any good bondage it liberates us from our freedom... Accept a game as a set of rules, then the Second Life world is a game, the player is tied painfully close to the limitations of network traffic and access points. As surplus to those limitations by the technological topography, a set of trading rules is superimposed by a game industry monopoly. Now the bond is strong enough that even businessmen, anti-tech hustlers and a Jedermann find SL equally attractive – for chatting and trading with each other, for sex and lollies."

With multi-model and multi-medium art group Second Front, the line between similitude and the multiple reals is ripe material. Performances by the group often centre around dividing the differences again and again; avatars watch videos from the real world, or dance around a portal connecting to footage from a real place. One of the SLebrities of the group, Man Michinaga (Patrick Lichty), occupies a life not dissimilar to that of artists in the new virtuality, squaring up against the tough circumstances of the city a hundred years ago. Scavenging for materials but never dry for inspiration, the Second Life artist quests like any other for situations to abstract.

Man Michinaga is an origami artist, true in shape and process but drenched in the paradox of not quite being there. Totally urbanised, but as feral and scavenging as any real person. Sneaking about the place looking for opportunities, code, friends. Others realise Second Life's potential and perverse appeal – like fellow Front member and mediated artist Scott Kildall. Second Front's movements are devout to the empyrean divide of the first and second worlds. On October 4th, 2007, the Front performed at Odyssey inside Second Life and Brussels, Belgium, a city already virtualised by its position in the global body politic. iMAL (Interactive Media Art Laboratory) was connected to "The Gate", a portal zone that spat a videofeed back to the Laboratory, while images from Brussels were spat back to The Gate. Acting less like a two-way mirror than a reflecting pool, people on both sides were happy to play with the ripples in the water and watch the stars dance.

Members of the troupe were arranged around and on the neo-baroque Gate, twitching, bleeping, clothes in flux. How exactly one can experience the performance is also in flux; is Second Life presence any more perfect an experience of a doubly-virtual scenario than a streaming video of the event? In watching performances such as that at The Gate, audiences are generally treated to a ritualised version of events already occurring in Second Life. The world is abundant, almost Olympian, populated by a race of excessive, outlandish avatars. The world as flattened fantasy zone, and the world as lived, bricked-in reality. This offers a dense plane of signs and meanings for artists to interpret; everything in a sense comes ready to be converted into art of some form. The Gate is an evolution of Rodin's *Gates of Hell*, a design originally meant to disavow constructed meanings and literally force the visitor to visit a kind of sculptural and kinetic hell before they could pass through. The magical threshold for Second Life is sculptural in a different sense, where artists can make images from both worlds connect, but the trick is to understand who precisely is travelling – player or avatar – and into precisely where.

NEVER VIRTUAL

Environmental architect R. Buckminster Fuller, knowing full well the trappings of utopian fervour, foregrounded the practical manifestations of errors and coincidence as design allegories. The history of virtual space, going back to pre-linguistic uses of gypsums and chalks to demarcate boundaries, bears out the narrative. We build in dreams. We learn to build in dreams. We build dreams through learning. And so on.

Technology and especially this monstrous phenomenon called virtuality was Fuller's bugbear; it was and still is powered not by metaphors but an existing history, going back to these first representational arts, by which we placed faith in exteriority to the self.

It is precisely their Second Life-ness which makes them zones of purest design and art. The properties of a world such as Second Life lend themselves to exploratory movements in design. The mutable avatars, capable of flight, are in a sense the perfect subjects of utopian architecture, with all the unintended consequences that entails. With no restrictions, the vernacular of space need no longer be vernacular.

To describe an environment such as Ars Virtua as a gallery is to already shortcut the densities and opportunities of Second Life art spaces. Fuller's notion springs to life here and everywhere that a zone of machinic design opens up. Ars Virtua is an engine-space, chewing through intuitions and artworks, audiences and permutations. The ability for the space to ephemeralise and create cross-world architectural art jokes is one of the more potent and positive instances of a living gallery to date.

The Bitfactory Exhibition Space.
SCREENSHOT BY RICHARDO PEACH

Avatars flowing through Adam Nash's sonic scapes.
SCREENSHOT BY RICHARDO PEACH

The avatars that question the technotopian ideal of "always young, always beautiful" are my favorites... the usual avatar, or worse yet, the remediation of the real life appearance, is completely at odds with the Linden rhetoric. In many ways, it is the well-known axiom of giving the starving person a vast menu and, not knowing what to order, they get a cheeseburger for its familiarity."

– *Patrick Lichty*

Brad Kligerman's AVAIR at Ars Virtua. Screenshot by Melinda Rackham.

Brad Kligerman's AVAIR residence in Second Life was an utterance of distance, an occupation with how virtual communities affect our personal ecologies and surrounding objects. His approach to the process of virtualised objects was to reignite the process we are already familiar with; built machines handle Calibration, Analogy and Mutation of data from Second Life to reinterpret and reuse existing materials already available. Our tour group dances and chats in Ars Virtua for some time.

> *Are we visiting art?*
> *Are our avatars' presence making art?*
> *Are we socialising?*

Spaces and buildings become reinterpreted data; spikes of colour and light flux and shift. The real mutation is not in the process of material uses, but in the process of their deployment in art. It is the art process which is being ephemeralised, not virtual space, or even real space. The events to promote the residency were, in every sense, the purpose of the residency. Kligerman's work transposes a concern for the uncanny everyday world into Second Life, into a world where uncanniness is in the soil and sea. Everyday objects for us literally take on new dimensions, or the rules of geometry shatter. The doubts and concerns about how to comprehend the role of art melted away into air.

Eva and Franco Mattes, *7000 Oaks Project*.
Screenshot by Christian McCrea

REMEDIATION

On March 16, 1982, artist Joseph Beuys began his work at the Documenta 7 festival, planting the first of his *7000 Oaks* in order to spread concern for the diminishing forestry on the once-green world. Each oak was paired with a freestanding basalt column, a ritual marker of importance that would be as legible to pre-lingual times as it would be in a wholly virtual sphere. Artists Eva and Franco Mattes took up the challenge to mirror the *7000 Oaks* project by distributing 7.000 trees and stones in Second Life on the twenty-fifth anniversary of Beuys' original project.

What does it mean for environmental, or land art for that matter, to be replicated in virtual worlds? The environmental scenario for a multi-user computer simulation is on the surface very bleak; thousands of hours of computer use go into a single hour of normal traffic in

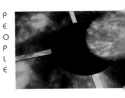

Eva and Franco Mattes *Shoot*
performance documentation
at Odyssey.
SCREENSHOT BY MELINDA RACKHAM

Second Life. Yet the Mattes' reworking of Beuys is never silent on the issue of the real, engaging with both the newly-ritualised process of "planting" and the twenty-five years since Beuys' original concern, in which his type of work could only be more urgent than ever.

The Mattes rearticulate important elements of twentieth-century art history by repositioning photography and collectorship at the centre of their virtual tourism. Their work on Thirteen *Most Beautiful Avatars* acknowledges the Warhol antecedent in process but in practice develops something altogether new. In a webcam-infested world, portraiture has an all-new reflexive action.

The remediation of Chris Burden's *Shoot at Odyssey* was performed and watched in-world, documented in-world and now documentation is displayed in-world as photographs or video stills on the Odyssey Gallery walls. The hilarity of this tripling and folding is not lost on an avatar audience, viewing a remediation of a remediation. Someone looks at something = Art.

HOPE SPRINGS ETERNAL

If Cocteau's famous dictum that film is a frozen fountain of time holds true, then our experiences of Second Life, bound by the aesthetic of the tour, with powers of flight and instant movement, could be the entire garden.

The life which is second produces meanings about the first even without drawing back the bleeping, erratic curtain. Those continually searching for a raison (or is that, "maison") d'etre for Second Life, wondering what the hype is all about, arrive in search of meaning in zones inhabited mostly by people looking for the same intensities, victories and pleasures, as well as the strivings, failings and flaws of the seedling art practices which exist in-world.

There is no grand surprise coming; the art phenomena of Second Life are articulating and rearticulating the art world's concerns at the same speed and register. It is not just art being simulated, but the life of the artist. If art serves to abstract in a different sense than simulation, not to model situations but to remove them from their context for a moment, then where art and simulation meet we find a zone totally at odds with itself. Artists fold space and time to turn them into a newness which accelerates our experience.

Simulations and games fold space and time to develop experiences which accelerate newness. The experiment-engine of Second Life offers potential; in a sense, that is all it offers. The tour residents undertake on every visit is a tourism utterly unlike the virtual worlds before it, or the game-worlds competing for the current clock cycles of our computers. A garden of errors, glitches and twitches offers the visitor, the dweller and the provocateur ample fruit for harvest.

THE ORIGINAL TOUR WAS CURATED BY SL RESIDENTS LYTHE WITTE (CHRISTY DENA), ANGRYBETH SHORTBREAD (ANNABETH ROBINSON), MAN MICHINAGA (PATRICK LICHTY), DOESI BECK (STEPHAN DOESINGER), RICARDO PARAVANE (RICARDO PEACH), BELLA BOUCHARD (KATHY CLELAND), ADAM RAMONA (ADAM NASH), AND RUBAIYAT SHATNER (JAMES MORGAN).
-EMPYRE- AUGUST 2007, FACILITATED BY MELINDA RACKHAM, HTTP://WWW.SUBTLE.NET/EMPYRE
THANK YOU TO DAVID CRANSWICK FOR WRANGLING THE D.LUX PONY CLUB PONIES, HTTP://WWW.DLUX.ORG.AU
MARGEURITE CHARMANTE'S "3RD LIFE PLAYSURE: TERTIUS ORBIS MEMORANDUM", LUDIC SOCIETY MAGAZINE, ISSUE 4

"There are your standard dwarves and gnomes and monsters; there is a whole heap of steampunk avatars, and some fantastic 3D animated sculptures that some people are using... a huge elven community, a mermaid community, the neko women, and the panther women, some goth and grunge, a very high number of queer folk, particularly gay, lesbian and transsexuals, and some of the most famous furries from the grid."

– *Angela Thomas*

The tour is over.
SCREENSHOT BY KATHY CLELAND.

BIBLIOGRAPHY

PAGES 30 – 45:
Barabási 2002   Albert László Barabási: Linked. The New Science of Networks. Perseus, Cambridge/MA 2002.

Bettencourt et al. 2007   Luís M. A. Bettencourt, José Lobo, Dirk Helbing, Christian Kühnert and Geoffrey B. West, 'Growth, innovation, scaling, and the pace of life in cities.' PNAS, April 24th, 2007; 104 (17): 7301–7306. Published online April 16th 2007. doi: 10.1073/pnas.0610172104.

Blake 1996   Peter Blake, No Place like Utopia. Modern Architecture and the Company We Kept. Norton, New York/London 1996.

Bogdanov 1989   Aleksandr Bogdanov, Der rote Planet. Ingenieur Menni. Utopische Romane. Verlag Volk und Welt, Berlin 1989 (original Russian title of the former: Krasnaja zvezda. Leningrad 1929).

Bredekamp 1994   Horst Bredekamp: 'Albertis Flug- und Flammenauge'. In: Die Beschwörung des Kosmos: europäische Bronzen der Renaissance. (ed. Christoph Brockhaus, revised by Gottlieb Leinz). Exhib. cat. Wilhelm Lehmbruck Museum 6.11.1994 - 15.1.1995. Duisburg 1994. p. 297ff.

Chua 2005   Leon O. Chua, 'Local Activity is the Origin of Complexity'. International Journal of Bifurcation and Chaos 15 (2005) 3435-3456. (DOI: 10.1142/S0218127405014337).

Der utopische Staat 1960   Der utopische Staat. Morus Utopia. Campanella Sonnenstaat. Bacon Neu-Atlantis. Ed. by Klaus J. Heinisch. (Philosophie des Humanismus und der Renaissance, vol. 3). Rowohlt, Reinbek bei Hamburg 1960.

Economist 2007   'Trouble in paradise. The banking crisis finds an echo in Second Life.' The Economist, August 16th, 2007 (URL: http://www.economist.com/finance/displaystory.cfm?story_id=9661900).

Elkins 2000   James Elkins, How to Use Your Eyes. Routledge, London 2000.

Érdi 2008   Péter Érdi, Complexity Explained. Sprinter, Berlin/ Heidelberg/New York 2008.

Freeman 2004   Linton Freeman, The Development of Social Network Analysis: A Study in the Sociology of Science. Empirical Press, Vancouver 2004.

Gibson 2005   William Gibson, Die Neuromancer-Trilogie. Neuromancer. Biochips. Mona Lisa Overdrive. Heyne, Munich 2005 (original American title: Neuromancer. New York 1984).

Gombrich 1960   Ernst H. Gombrich, Art & Illusion. Phaidon, London/New York 1960/1977 (reprint 1996).

Gombrich 1979   Ernst H. Gombrich, The Sense of Order. Phaidon, London/

New York 1979/1984 (reprint 2002). Le Corbusier Jeanneret 1957-65   Le Corbusier, Pierre Jeanneret: Oeuvre complète. (ed.: Willy Boesiger. Girsberger, Zurich 1957-1965, vol. 7).

Le Corbusier 1960   Le Corbusier, Mein Werk. Hatje, Stuttgart 1960.

Müller 2007   Markus Müller, Second Life. Data Becker, Düsseldorf 2007.

Pehnt 1983   Wolfgang Pehnt, 'Rasterpraxis und Proportionslehre. Raster und Modul im 19. und frühen 20. Jahrhundert.' in: Der Anfang der Bescheidenheit. Kritische Aufsätze zur Architektur des 20. Jahhunderts. Munich 1983, pp. 19-41.

Saage 1991   Richard Saage, Politische Utopien der Neuzeit. Wissenschaftliche Buchgesellschaft, Darmstadt 1991.

Schich 2007   Maximilian Schich, 'Rezeption und Tradierung als komplexes Netzwerk. Der CENSUS und visuelle Dokumente zu den Thermen in Rom.' Diss. Humboldt University, Berlin 2007 (preprint available: http://www.schich.info).

Second Life Wiki s.v. Custom Linden Plants, Second Life Wiki contributors, 'Custom Linden Plants', Second Life Wiki, https://wiki.secondlife.com/w/index.php?title=Custom_Linden_Plants&oldid=16209 (accessed October 17th, 2007).

SL handbook 2007   Michael Rymaszewski, Second Life. Das offizielle Handbuch. Trsl. from English by Judith Muhr. WILEY-VCH, Weinheim 2007.

Spiegel 2007, 'Alles im Wunderland'. Article from Spiegel 8, 2007, 17.02.2007, pp. 150-163.

Sterling 1988   Bruce Sterling, Islands in the Net. Arbor House, New York 1988.

Summers 2003   David Summers, Real Spaces. World Art History and the Rise of Western Modernism. Phaidon, London/ New York 2003.

Wigley 2001   Mark Wigley, Network Fever. Grey Room, summer 2001, no. 04, pp. 82-122, posted online March 13th, 2006. (DOI: 10.1162/152638101750420825).

Wikipedia s.v. Computer Cluster Wikipedia contributors, 'Computer cluster,' Wikipedia, The Free Encyclopedia, http://en.wikipedia.org/w/index.php?title=Computer_cluster&oldid=164431487 (accessed October 17, 2007).

Wikipedia s.v. Grid-Computing   Wikipedia contributors, 'Grid computing', Wikipedia, The Free Encyclopedia, http://en.wikipedia.org/w/index.php?title=Grid_computing&oldid=163774507 (accessed October 17, 2007).

Wikipedia s.v. Metaverse, Wikipedia contributors, 'Metaverse,' Wikipedia, The Free Encyclopedia, http://en.wikipedia.org/w/

index.php?title=Metaverse&oldid=165003005 (accessed October 17, 2007). Wikipedia s.v. MMORPG, Wikipedia contributors, 'Massively multiplayer online role-playing game,' Wikipedia, The Free Encyclopedia, http://en.wikipedia.org/w/index.php?title=Massively_multiplayer_online_role-playing_game&oldid=165081188 (accessed October 17, 2007).

IMAGES:

PAGE 3:
Baston
http://www.flickr.com/photos/baston/34678884/
Creative Commons

PAGE 4 – 5:
Competition entry by David Denton

PAGE 6 – 7:
Tor Lindstrand & LOL architects

PAGES 30 – 45:

Page 30: The Second Life Logo photo: Linden Research Inc., 2007; for logo, see: http://static.secondlife.com/downloads/logos.zip; for info, see: secondlife.com s.v. Trademark Usage: http://secondlife.com/corporate/trademark/print_web.php

Page 30: The Eye Woodcut from Horapollo, Paris 1551. From: Bredekamp 1994, ill. 3, p. 298.

Page 31: Le Corbusier: The Open Hand photo: Lucien Hervé, Paris. From: Le Corbusier, Pierre Jeanneret: Oeuvre complète. (ed. by Willy Boesiger. Girsberger, Zurich 1957-1965, vol. 7, p. 109 bottom right).

Page 32: Piranesi From: Hans Volkmann, Giovanni Battista Piranesi. Architekt und Graphiker. Verlag Bruno Hessling, Berlin 1965, ill. 13.

Page 33: City prospect from Urbino photo: Susan Tobin. From: Eric M. Zafran: Fifty Old Master Paintings from the Walters Art Gallery. Walters Art Gallery, Baltimore/Md 1988. ill., p. 43.

Page 33: De Chirico photo: Giuseppe Schiavinotto, Rome. From: Maurizio Calvesi (ed.): De Chirico: la nuova metafisica. Exhib. cat., Palazzo dei Congressi e delle Esposizioni 27.4.-27.9.1995 San Marino. De Luca, Rome 1995. Dipinti no. 1.

Pages 34 – 35: Andrea Pozzo's ceiling fresco in the church of Sant' Ignazio in Rome. Photo by Maximilian Schich, 2007.

Page 36: Le Corbusier, Primärkörper From: Le Corbusier, Ausblick auf eine

Architektur. Vieweg-Verlag, Brunswick 1982, p. 123 (original French title: Vers une Architecture. Paris 1923).

Page 36: Dürer. From: Albrecht Dürer, Das gesamte graphische Werk 1471 bis 1528. Handzeichnungen. Verlag Rogner & Bernhard, Munich 1971, vol. 1, ill. 475.

Page 36: Thamugadi. From: Bernard Andreae, Römische Kunst. Herder, Freiburg/Basle/Vienna 1973, ill. 836, p. 605.

Page 37: Stephen Wolfram, photo: Wolfram Media Inc. From: Stephen Wolfram, A New Kind of Science. Wolfram Media Inc., Champaign/IL 2001, ill. p. 400.

Page 37: Neapolitan nativity Photo: Jörg Hesse. From: Roberto Ubbidiente, Vincenzo De Lucia (eds.), Paradies der Kontraste: die neapolitanische Krippe. Exhib. cat., Staatliche Museen, Berlin 28.11.2003-1.2.2004. Waxmann, Münster etc. 2003, ill. p. 186 top.

Page 37: Pompeii photo: Mimmo Jodice, © Banco di Napoli. From: Fausto Zevi (ed.), Pompei. Guida Editori, Naples 1992, p. 233.

Page 38: Archigram/Ron Herron Collage from Gallery Project for Bournemouth, 1968, p. 337, Vision der Moderne – Das Prinzip Konstruktion, edited by Heinrich Klotz, Prestel, 1986.

Page 39: roxeteer / Visa Kopu, www.visakopu.net/ Licensed Creative Commons, http://www.flickr.com/photos/roxeteer/56645184/

Page 40: Sir Thomas More Virgilio Vercelloni, Atlante storico della città ideale, dell' idea Europea. Editoriale Jaca Book, Milan 1994, pl. 53.

Page 42: Le Corbusier: La Ville Radieuse Thilo Hilpert (ed.): Le Corbusiers 'Charta von Athen'. Texte und Dokumente. Vieweg-Verlag, Brunswick/Wiesbaden 1988, p. 230f.

Page 42: Ludwig Hilberseimer Vittorio Magnago Lampugnani and Romana Schneider (eds.): Moderne Architektur in Deutschland 1900 bis 1950. Expressionismus und Neue Sachlichkeit. Exhib. cat., Verlag Gerd Hatje, Stuttgart 1994, ill. p. 189, bottom.

Page 43: Mike Slichenmyer http://www.flickr.com/photo_zoom.gne?id=117564634&size=o Creative Commons

Page 43: Brazil. Still from Terry Gilliam (director), Brazil. UK 1984. Twentieth Century Fox Home Entertainment DVD 2003.

Page 44: Richard Buckminster-Fuller James Ward (ed.), The artifacts of R. Buckminster Fuller: a comprehensive collection of his designs and drawings in 4 vol. Vol. 4: 'The Geodesic Revolution', Part II, 1960-1983. Garland, New York etc. 1985. ill. p. 218 top.

JURY MEMBERS:

SHUMON BASAR, writer, editor, curator, director of AACP at the Architectural Association, London
MATHIEU WELLNER, facilitator of architecture, Haus der Kunst and Pinakothek der Moderne, Munich
TOR LINDSTRAND, architect, International Festival and Royal Institute of Technology, Stockholm
PASCAL SCHÖNING, author and architect, Unit Master at the Architectural Association, London
DR MELINDA RACKHAM, Executive Director, Australian Network for Art and Technology (ANAT)
STEPHAN DOESINGER, artist, creative director & architect, initiator of the competition, Munich

WEBLINKS:

The competition:
www.sl-award.com

Stephan Doesinger:
www.doesinger.com

Ars Electronica:
www.aec.at

Zollverein Essen:
www.zollverein.de

ACKNOWLEDGEMENTS: The author would like to express his thanks to all the members of the jury and to all contributers, to Jürgen Krieger, Curt Holtz & Katharina Haderer at Prestel Verlag, Christine Schöpf, Gerfried Stocker & Martin Honzik at Ars Electronica, Roland Weiss, Corinne Valentin & Claudia Radinger at Entwicklungsgesellschaft Zollverein Essen, Modulorbeat, Tuncay Acar, Milan Grbovic, Helmuth Gsöllpointner, Kristian Fenzl, Christian Olsson, Dominik Mayer, Lisa Bartl, Florian Schömer, Christiane Pfau, Patricia Dittmar (Octane PR), Rowan Barnett, Markus Bokowsky. Special thanks to: Johanna & David.

The 1st Annual Architecture & Design Competition was made possible through the support of Ligne Roset and Südhausbau.
Media partner: The Avastar (www.avastar.de)

ARCHITECTURE IS VISIBLE THINKING.

SÜD
HAUS
BAU

WWW.SUEDHAUSBAU.DE

Zeichen & Wunder